SELECTED INDUSTRIAL POLICY INSTRUMENTS

Objectives and Scope

This report on selected industrial policy instruments was approved by the Industry Committee at its 31st session.

The decision to derestrict the report was taken by the Council on 9th November 1977.

ORGANISATION FOR ECONOMIC CO-OPERATION AND DEVELOPMENT

The Organisation for Economic Co-operation and Development (OECD) was set up under a Convention signed in Paris on 14th December 1960, which provides that the OECD shall promote policies designed:

- to achieve the highest sustainable economic growth and employment and a rising standard of living in Member countries, while maintaining financial stability, and thus to contribute to the development of the world economy;
- to contribute to sound economic expansion in Member as well as non-member countries in the process of economic development;
- to contribute to the expansion of world trade on a multilateral, non-discriminatory basis in accordance with international obligations.

The Members of OECD are Australia, Austria, Belgium, Canada, Denmark, Finland, France, the Federal Republic of Germany, Greece, Iceland, Ireland, Italy, Japan, Luxembourg, the Netherlands, New Zealand, Norway, Portugal, Spain, Sweden, Switzerland, Turkey, the United Kingdom and the United States.

TABLE OF CONTENTS

Part II

PROMOTION OF STRUCTURAL ADAPTATION

Part III

THE SPECIAL CASE OF SMALL AND MEDIUM-SIZED FIRMS

Chapter 9

Part IV

5

Chapter I

GENERAL INTRODUCTION

A. INTRODUCTION

In response to people's varied aspirations, the public authorities have gradually assumed responsibility for an increasing number of facets of economic activity - although the speed and extent of this process vary considerably from one country to another - and this trend has been accompanied by the development and establishment of instruments enabling them to meet these responsibilities, in particular with regard to industry. The main purpose of industrial policy instruments is to permit the transfer of resources between the State and industry in order to achieve specific objectives. This flow can and moreover does move in both directions, i.e. enterprises help to finance public expenditure and can also receive capital transfers. Because of the variety of existing instruments and the complex effects they produce, it is necessary to draw up a table of the financial flows between the State and industry in order to be in a position to assess their scale, direction and, if need be and if possible, effectiveness.

This report is based on information received from 16 Member countries: Australia, Belgium, Canada, Denmark, Finland, France, Germany, Greece, Italy, Japan, New Zealand, Norway, Portugal, Spain, Sweden and the United Kingdom. These countries submitted their information at different stages in the conception of the study and the report, and this splitting-up may have had consequences as regards the homogeneity and comparability of the data; however, the bulk of the information was provided during the period between the middle of 1974 and the beginning of 1975. The present report is intended to take account of the comments and amendments submitted both orally (during a meeting of a group of experts on 5th-6th May, 1975) and in writing. Updating information to cover the year 1975 has been submitted by Belgium, Germany, Japan, Spain and the United Kingdom, and has been integrated in the report as appropriate.

B. OBJECT OF THE REPORT

The purpose of the study, as originally defined, is as follows:

1. To determine the extent to which countries have developed specific industrial policy instruments, and the objectives assigned to each instrument or group of instruments;
2. To determine the circumstances which led to the development of the different types of instruments and the rationale motivating the choice of each specific instrument;
3. To determine the nature of the various instruments used and, if funded, the nature and sources of funding (budgetary, capital market or deposits);
4. To determine the extent to which the instruments available are effectively used and by whom;
5. To determine the effectiveness of these instruments, by examining the objectives assigned to them, and the extent to which they have contributed to the achievement of these objectives.

C. SCOPE OF THE REPORT

Industrial policy instruments are not only extremely varied, as was said above, they are also very numerous. This is mainly for two reasons. In the first place, industrial activity does not depend only on industrial policy and the relevant instruments; it is also influenced by incentives or constraints deriving from other areas of government activity: political, economic, environmental, technological, etc. Secondly, the content of industrial policy varies from country to country depending, for example, on whether it includes government purchasing.

To begin with, therefore, an attempt had to be made to reduce the number and variety of instruments to more manageable proportions. As emerges from Item 1 above, the first limitation arose from the choice of objectives considered important in the context of the present report. These objectivs have been divided into two groups:

a) the promotion of productive investment and assistance for structural adaptation; and
b) increasing the efficiency of small and medium-sized enterprises and helping them to adjust.

Another limitation stemmed from the fact that only instruments depending strictly on central government were taken into account. Consequently, in countries with federal systems, instruments wielded by provinces, Länder or various local authorities were not included.

It must be stressed at this point that although this limitation is justified for practical reasons concerning the size of the study, it can in the case of federal countries result in the exclusion of substantial transfers of resources. In addition, because of the restrictive approach adopted, transfers effected via certain semi-public mixed economy or even private bodies (public enterprises, for example) have in general also been left out of consideration. The rules governing the working and activities of such bodies often allow them to exist independently of the public authorities.

A third major limitation is due to the nature of the instruments considered. Transfers of resources between the State and industry depend mainly on the following operations: transactions in goods and services such as equity holdings or public contracts; redistribution by budgetary means such as direct taxation or subsidies, and credit operations such as loans and guarantees. As far as the first objective is concerned, i.e. the promotion of productive investment and assistance for structural adaptation, the report will be confined to fiscal and financial instruments(1), whereas in the case of the second objective, i.e. increasing the efficiency of small and medium-sized enterprises and helping them to adapt, instruments of an "advisory" nature are added to those mentioned earlier.

D. ORGANISATION OF THE REPORT

The Instruments

Industrial policy instruments are the means used by the public authorities to influence the behaviour of enterprises in relation to targets fixed, in some cases, as part of a given strategy. These instruments are intended above all to influence either the profitability prospects of investment or operating conditions in enterprises by transferring financial costs or resources. An illustration of a transfer of costs is the case where an activity involving research into a manufacturing process is undertaken by and under the responsibility of the public authorities on behalf of a given industry. In fact, any credit transaction is an example of a transfer of financial resources.

These instruments have for the most part been developed as the responsibilities of the public authorities have expanded in response to people's growing expectations and forced them as a result to find means enabling them to intervene. Often they have been introduced in answer to given situations in industry, without necessarily being

---

1) For the purposes of this report, holdings taken in the equity of private enterprises by the State or by bodies which are government financed or managed are considered to be financial instruments.

incorporated in an overall strategy. The industrial problems to
which these instruments were intended to provide a solution were
themselves often very complex in that their cyclical or structural
origin, for example, was not obvious and differed from country to
country; consequently, the instruments themselves had to be complex
and varied in order to be suitable.

Depending on their point of impact, industrial policy instruments may be classified in different categories ranging from the
most general to the most specific. There can be instruments for
general application which are accessible to all industrial enterprises irrespective of size, activity, sector or geographic location
and, above all, which are not subject to prior authorisation based
on the examination of a supporting file or, in particular, bound up
with a government policy responsible for the introduction of the
relevant instrument. However, as each of the above factors can be
made a more or less restrictive condition, so the instrument concerned can be applied to a varying number of enterprises. Obviously,
the number of restrictive criteria possible is infinite, so that it
was necessary for the purpose of this study to introduce a different
classification which, in line with the object of the present paper,
would make it possible to investigate the effectiveness of the instruments. An attempt has therefore been made to classify the
instruments according to the objectives they were designed to fulfill.

The Objectives

Because of the inherent difficulties of classifying all the
objectives and of constructing a logical and if possible comprehensive
framework, it was thought preferable to take only a limited but essential number of objectives, not in order of importance but chosen
in the light of different countries' experiences, and distinguishing
between the promotion of productive investment and assistance for
structural adaptation. The objectives peculiar to small and medium-
sized enterprises have been dealt with separately.

Drawing a boundary between promoting investment and assisting
structural adaptation may in some ways seem specious in that, depending for example on the sense given to structural adaptation,
investment aid can be one way of promoting structural adaptation.
It is necessary to distinguish between the question of substance,
i.e. what is structural adaptation, and the empirical aspect, i.e.
what do countries understand by the concepts in question. In the
absence of a logical order of importance of the objectives and of
precise definitions for each of them, this question can doubtless
only be clarified by referring to usage in different countries.
However, it transpires that the concept of adjustment varies from
country to country, and also depends on the cause initially thought

to be behind the obligation to adjust and, consequently, on the proportion of industry in general affected by this obligation. Some countries in fact distinguish between the promotion of investment in the broad sense, as consistent with the healthy development of industry, whereas the concept of "structural adaptation" is confined in these countries to programmes intended either to concentrate resources in certain peak industries or to help industries with adjustment difficulties - often caused by increased competition from imports.

It may also be noted that the range of objectives chosen necessarily involved a process of selection in the course of which some objectives were abandoned because it was generally felt that they were not relevant to the aims and scope of the study.

The Instruments and the Objectives

In order to have a better grasp of the impact of the instruments on industrial activity, it would admittedly have been preferable to know what instruments are expected to achieve what particular objectives - if only for practical reasons concerning subsequent analyses. However, this is extremely difficult. In the first place, a number of instruments can be designed to achieve the same objective, just as one instrument can have several objectives at the same time - and this occurs all the more frequently when the objectives are not in logical order. An example of one objective pursued by several instruments at once is productive investment, the promotion of which can imply first of all that several fiscal instruments are being used simultaneously to encourage self-financing: accelerated depreciation and differential rates of tax on profits. However, there may also be financial instruments, such as loan guarantees for example, with the same objective. To try to note the effect of each of these instruments would be like trying to reason in terms of "all other things being equal", and this is an approach to be used with caution in an area where the impact of industrial policy instruments becomes confused with the effects of economic policies and economic mechanisms for encouraging or discouraging investment by entrepreneurs. This does not, on the other hand, prevent research into the volume of resources transferred from the State to industry and vice-versa.

Reference has been made above to the pragmatic and gradual development over a fairly long period of the industrial policy instruments considered in this report. In the course of their development, most of the instruments were modified as regards both the ways in which they were applied and the objectives they were intended to pursue.

E. DIAGRAMMATIC SUMMARY OF THE INFORMATION

From a first scrutiny of replies from the various countries it has been possible to draw up Tables I and II entitled, respectively: "Objectives of fiscal and financial instruments designed to promote productive investment and to facilitate structural adaptation" and "Objectives of instruments designed to increase the efficiency of small and medium-sized enterprises and to facilitate their adjustment".

From the first of these two tables it is clear that most countries make it their business to facilitate productive investment. This in no way means that for each individual country this objective is the primary one. This point will be examined at a later stage. All that can be said is that it is the most common of the objectives since all the replies refer to it.

Structural adaptation dictated by the continuous and in some ways accelerated state of change in present-day economies is assisted in most countries by enterprise-oriented rather than employment-oriented instruments. But this does not necessarily imply that, for each country, structural adaptation is mainly promoted by providing incentives to firms. Table I shows merely that more than 75 per cent of replies indicate this as one of the objectives of industrial policy, whereas hardly half of the countries use instruments with the employment situation in mind.

Table II is included because many countries recognise that the small and medium-sized enterprises located in their territory have characteristics which set them apart from larger enterprises and which, in the eyes of the authorities, justify and necessitate policies peculiar to this type of enterprise.

In most countries, three major objectives seem to be pursued in order to help small and medium-sized firms increase their efficiency and adapt to change. These major objectives affect the firm's economic or financial environment or legal status, the firm itself, or the people working in it. The introduction of new technical processes or products is the most frequent objective. All countries mention it; it directly affects the firm itself. Providing easier access to capital seems necessary both to give such firms a broader financial platform and to meet their investment requirements while bearing in mind the specific nature of the risk incurred. Most countries recognise this. In the case of small and medium-sized firms, therefore, it is primarily in the economic, financial and, sometimes, legal spheres that adjustment is usually needed. Lastly, staff training and information is important in firms small enough to be run by one or only very few persons. Training in management techniques would therefore appear to be essential in many respects if such firms are to develop.

These are the main objectives found most frequently in the replies given by the various countries. The means by which attempts
are made to achieve them are summarised in Tables III and IV. These
tables have been drawn up from information given in all the country
replies, each country being identified by the code letters used for
international motor traffic or by some similar method. They are
entitled: Table III - Fiscal and financial instruments designed to
promote productive investment and to facilitate structural adaptation
in all countries; Table IV - Instruments designed to increase the
efficiency of small and medium-sized enterprises and to facilitate
their adjustment in all countries.

From Table III it is clear that many countries appear to give
preference to either fiscal or financial instruments in order to
promote productive investment. The fiscal technique of accelerated
depreciation seems to be that most regularly used in order to promote
the extension of production capacity. Ten countries refer to it in
their replies. Admittedly, it is not the only instrument used, and
in many countries credit facilities of all kinds and grants also contribute to the same end. They would appear, however, to be less
generally used than the former technique.

Conversely, countries are more inclined to give grants when it
is a matter of promoting the introduction of new products or processes. The need for R and D in order to achieve this objective has
led many countries to bear part of the risk involved in such activities increasingly as an ultimate State responsibility, that is to
say by non-repayable grants when necessary. Initially, assistance
was given in individual cases or to individual industries - the
advanced technology industries for example - but nowadays it is
tending to cover all spheres of industrial activity. Other forms of
incentive involving a reduction in the risk borne by businesses are
also used: easier credit by means of loans at concessionary rates
of interest, and the fiscal technique of accelerated depreciation.

In order to promote structural adaptation, which is also an
objective for many countries, financial instruments seem to be pre-
ferred in many cases. The spectrum of possibilities is very broad,
ranging from grants to loan guarantees depending on the specific
purpose in mind, as will be seen later on in this study.

For countries that have introduced as part of their industrial
policy mechanisms designed to redeploy manpower allowances and grants
paid either to enterprises or to workers themselves continue in most
cases to be the only methods commonly employed.

Table IV shows that, in order to achieve the main objective in
the case of small and medium-sized enterprises, most countries pre-
fer to use financial or service-type instruments as opposed to fiscal
techniques whose differential application in relation to the size

Table I.   AIMS OF POLICIES DESIGNED TO PROMOTE PRODUCTI

COUNTRIES

PRIMARY AIMS

1. Extension of capacity

2. Creation of employment

3. Introduction of new products and processes

4. Others (to be specified)

A. Company-oriented instruments

5. Diversification/conversion

6. Modernisation/rationalization

7. Productivity/capacity (including creation of enterprises)

8. Concentration/integration (including the disappearance of enterprises)

9. Co-operation/association

10. Others (to be specified)

B. Manpower-oriented instruments

11. Income guarantee

12. Geographical mobility

13. Occupational mobility

14. Others (to be specified)

Note: Countries are identified with their international car registration plate or a
      similar device:

D	=	Germany	I	=	Italy
AUS	=	Australia	N	=	Norway
B	=	Belgium	NZ	=	New Zealand
CDN	=	Canada	P	=	Portugal
DK	=	Denmark	GB	=	United Kingdom
E	=	Spain	S	=	Sweden
SF	=	Finland	J	=	Japan
GR	=	Greece			

D	A US	B	C ND	D K	E	S F	G R	I	N	N Z	P	G B	S	J	
				I. PROMOTION OF PRODUCTIVE INVESTMENT											
*	*	*	*	*	*	*	*	*		*	*	*	*	*	
*	*	*	*		*	*	*			*		*	*		
*	*	*	*	*	*	*		*	*	*	*	*	*	*	
	*	*	*			*	*	*	*	*	*		*	*	
				II. STRUCTURAL ADAPTATION											
*	*	*	*			*		*	*		*	*	*	*	
*	*	*	*	*	*	*		*	*		*	*	*	*	
*	*	*	*		*	*		*	*		*	*	*	*	
*	*		*	*	*		*	*	*			*	*	*	
*				*	*				*				*	*	
*	*		*		*	*	*						*	*	
*	*							*					*		
*	*		*			*						*	*		
*	*		*			*		*			*	*	*		
*	*					*						*			

of the firm is difficult. As many countries point out, their taxation systems are uniform and take no account of the special nature of small and medium-sized enterprises. The fiscal instrument is therefore relatively little used.

In terms of the three most commonly pursued objectives (cf Table II), i.e.: the introduction of new technical processes and new products; access to capital, and training in management techniques, one arrives at the following conclusions: to facilitate the introduction of new products and technical processes, most countries provide advice and information for small and medium-sized enterprises. Access to capital is made easier by credit facilities and in particular by loans at concessionary rates or by governmental guarantees. Countries indicating that individual improvement in management skills is one of their objectives implement this policy by training and advice, but some countries point out that this aspect of their industrial policy is not a function of the size of the firm concerned.

F. USE OF INSTRUMENTS

The existence of a policy instrument or instruments, apparently conceived with reference to the problem or problems to which they are expected to provide a solution, is not in itself a guarantee that they will be used successfully. An important consideration as regards the effective use of an instrument by all the enterprises which qualify is that it should be suited to the requirements peculiar to the management of enterprises. This implies that the instrument should be fairly easily accessible, i.e. that procedures for examining files should be relatively simple, which is itself bound up with the time taken over decisions to make allocations (these factors can be of some importance for small enterprises). It also supposes a certain correlation between the financial resources available and the nature and scale of the problem to be solved and, lastly, recognition of the need to avoid conceptions entailing management costs (as regards accounting, for example) out of proportion to the advantages that an enterprise may derive from using a given instrument, both when preparing the file and when possibly checking the application of the instrument subsequent to the decision to allocate it.

Table II

AIMS OF POLICIES DESIGNED TO INCREASE EFFICIENCY AND FACILITATE ADAPTATION OF S.M.B.'s

COUNTRIES / PRIMARY AIDS	D	AUS	B	CDN	DK	E	SF	GR	I	N	NZ	P	GB	S	J
15. Access to capital	*	*	*	*	*	*	*	*	*	*	*		*	*	*
16. Introduction of new processes, techniques	*	*	*	*	*	*	*	*	*	*	*	*	*	*	*
17. Product marketing: on the home market; on the international market	*	*	*				*			*	*	*	*	*	*
18. Concentration/integration - Co-operation/association	*		*						*	*		*	*	*	*
19. Creation of technology - base enterprises		*	*	*			*		*		*			*	*
20. Training of management in management techniques	*	*	*				*		*	*	*	*	*	*	*
21. Employment of highly qualified manpower		*	*				*		*			*	*		*
22. Access to and participation in Government contracts	*										*				*
23. Position vis-à-vis bigger enterprises	*		*					*					*		*
24. Compliance with administrative or regulatory requirements									*			*	*	*	*
25. Others (specify)	*	*		*			*	*	*				*	*	*

Note: See Table 1.

17

Table III   UTI

INSTRUMENTS / PRIMARY AIMS	Accelerated Depreciation	Investment Reserves	Tax Credits
I. PROMOTION OF PRODUCTIVE INVESTMENT			
1. Extension of capacity (1)	B-CDN-DK-E SF-GR-I-J- NZ-GB-S	DK-E-SF-NZ P-S	AUS-E
2. Creation of employment	B-CDN-E-GR GB-S	SF-S	AUS-E
3. Introduction of new products and processes	D-AUS-CDN E-J-GB-S	P	E-J
4. Other (to be specified)	AUS-B-CDN GR-P	SF-J-P-S	GR-NZ
II. STRUCTURAL ADAPTATION			
A. Company oriented Instruments			
5. Diversification/conversion	D-B-J	S	D
6. Modernisation/rationalisation	D-B-CDN-E SF-J	DK-E	D-E
7. Productivity/capacity extension (1)	D-B-CDN-E SF-J	E-SF	D-E
8. Concentration/integration (2)	E		E
9. Co-operation/association			E
10. Other (to be specified)	D	SF	
B. Manpower oriented instruments			
11. Income guarantee			
12. Geographical mobility			
13. Occupational mobility (3)		SF	
14. Other (to be specified)			

1) Including the creation of enterprises.
2) Including the disappearance of enterprises.
3) Such as training qualification etc.
Note: See Table I.

Financial instruments

r advances		State participation (b)		Other (specify)
Guaranteed (a)	Other (specify)	direct	indirect	
D-AUS-B CDN-NZ-S	S	E-P-GB	B-SF-NZ	AUS
D-AUS-B NZ	S	AUS-E-GB	AUS-B-SF NZ	AUS
AUS-CDN DK-J-NZ		E-NZ-P GB	SF-NZ	GB
AUS-B			NZ	
D-AUS-B CDN-N		N	B-SF	
D-AUS-B-CDN DK-J-N-S		N-GB	B-SF	
D-AUS-B CDN-N		E-N	B-SF	
AUS-CDN-N		N-GB		AUS
J-N-S		N		
S	CDN	E		
		AUS	AUS	
		AUS-GB	AUS	
		AUS-P-GB	AUS	
AUS				

private bodies.
in the registered capital of a new company.

Table IV   UTILISATIOⁿ

INSTRUMENTS / PRIMARY AIMS	Fiscal Instruments			Financial		
Instruments designed to promote/ improve/ simplify	Accelerated Depreciation	Profits or losses	Other (specify)	Grants or premiums	At commercial rates (Direct)	At r
15. Access to capital	B-NZ		B	B	AUS-CND	
16. The introduction of new processes, techniques or their improvement	NZ		GR-P	D-E	SF-J	

17. Product marketing
  - on the home market
  - on the international market
	B-P
	N-Z
		NZ-J	AUS-B
			P
				AUS-
				NZ
				S
					SF-J	

18. Concentration/integration - co-operation/ association	B-J	J	B-P	D-S	J	
19. Creation of technology based enterprises	B-NZ		B-P		J	
20. Training of management in management techniques		P		NZ-S	J	
21. Employment of highly trained manpower	B	P	B	AUS-B	J	
22. Access to and partici- pation in government contracts					J	
23. Position vis-à-vis bigger enterprises		J	GR		J	
24. The compliance with administrative or regulatory requirements					J	
25. Other (specify)		GR	P	AUS	AUS-J	

(a) Including those cases where the principal is provided by private bodies.

(b) "State participation" refers to any public shareholding in the registered capital of a company.

Note: See Table I.

Profits or losses	Other (specify)	Grants premiums allowances indemnities	Credit facilities, loans direct at commercial rates	at reduced rates	interest subsidised (a)
I-S	D-B-CDN-SF-P	D-B-NZ-GB-S	AUS-CDN-NZ P-S	D-AUS-E-NZ P-GB	AUS-B-SF NZ-GB
S	D-B-CDN	D-B-SF-GB S-CDN	AUS-NZ-S	D-AUS-E-GB	AUS-B-SF NZ-GB
	D-CDN-J P	D-AUS-CDN NZ-J-GB-S	AUS-CDN-SF NZ-P	D-AUS-B-E-I J-N-P-GB	SF-NZ
	AUS-CDN SF-GR-P	AUS-SF GR-N-NZ-S	AUS-P-NZ	AUS-I-P	B-SF-GR
	D-B-J-P	D-AUS-B CDN-N	AUS-CDN-SF N-P-GB	D-AUS-I-P	B
	D-B-CDN SF-P	D-AUS-B CDN-N-S	AUS-CDN-SF N-P-GB	D-AUS-E I-P	B-CDN-SF
	D-B-CDN SF-P	D-AUS-B SF-CDN-N GB	AUS-CDN-SF N-P	D-AUS-E I-P-GB	B-CDN-SF GB
GR-I-S	DK-J-P	D-AUS-S	AUS-CDN-N GB	AUS	
	DK	D-S	J-N	J	S
	SF-GR-P	D-SF	SF	J	GR-S
		D-I-S			
		D-CDN-GB		D	SF
P		D-AUS-CDN SF-I		D	
		D-SF-GB	AUS	D-AUS	

a) Including those cases where the principal is provided by
b) "State participation" refers to any public shareholding

Instruments							
Credit facilities, loans or advances				State participation (b)		Other (specify)	Counselling
reduced rates	Interest (a) subsidised	Guaranteed(a)	Other (specify)	Direct	Indirect		
D-AUS-DK SF-I-N- GB-S	B-SF	B-CDN-SF- GR-I-J- N-S		SF-J	B-SF-I GB-S	SF	CDN-I N-GB-S
B-UK-SF- N-GB	SF	D-SF GR-J-N	S	SF	SF-GB-S		D-AUS CDN-SF I-J-N GB-S
B-SF	B	B-J N-S			B-GB		D-B-SF- I-N-NZ- GB-S
D-I N	B	B-J N-S			B		D-B I-GB
	B	B-J		SF	B-SF		I-NZ
SF-J		J		SF NZ	SF-NZ GB		B-SF I-J-N NZ-GB-S
SF	B	B-J			B-GB		I-GB
		J			GB		I-NZ
		J					B-I J-GB
		J					I-GB
D-SF-GB		J					CDN-I GB

Service-type instruments				Administrative and regulatory instruments	Other (specify)
formation	Training	Technical Assistance	Other (specify)		
CDN-N GB-S	CDN-N	N-GB			
D-CDN SF-J N-GB S	D-SF N-GB S	AUS-SF J-N GB-S			
B-SF-J- N-NZ- GB-S	B-SF N-GB S	AUS-B SF-N GB	AUS	J-NZ	
D-B	B	B			
		AUS-I			
B-SF J-N GB-S	D-AUS-B CDN-SF-I N-GB-S	B-N			
GB	I-J GB	J-GB			
NZ-GB		NZ		D	J
B-J GB	B	B		J	D
GB	GB				
AUS GB				GB	J

G. IMPACT OF THE INSTRUMENTS

There are three types of difficulty involved in considering the impact of industrial policy instruments: identification, measurement and, lastly, impact.

At the identification stage, it is mainly a question of being able to isolate the effects of industrial policy instruments from those which may occur through other types of government action and from those which may result from the influence of the general economic environment. An example is the case of investment and its long-term development in a given sector and the possible effect of a policy of price controls as part of counter-inflation policy, of an uncertain cyclical situation and, lastly, of the existence of a series of tax incentives to encourage investment.

At the measurement stage, the main problem is the comparability of the different instruments. The question is to find a common denominator between, for example, the advantages that may be derived from accelerated depreciation and an interest subsidy on a long-term loan discounted at the present time. This denominator could be the subsidy-equivalent. This technique,which is valuable in the case of financial instruments, can have serious drawbacks in the case of fiscal instruments, for which it is difficult to find a situation that could be considered "normal" and which could be used as a reference because of the bilateral nature of the flows and the variety of different situations.

In trying to measure the cascade effect between an enterprise and other sectors of industrial and economic life, the difficulty lies in the relative autonomy or independence of the various decision-making centres. The scale and distribution of the impact depend first of all on the behaviour of the enterprise which is the main beneficiary of any advantages that a particular instrument may give. An example is the case of investment aid. Depending on the behaviour of the enterprise, the advantages can be broken down in various ways, depending on whether the advantage obtained, i.e. the surplus created, is distributed inside the enterprise or passed on to a customer through a direct or indirect action on prices. One factor which can influence this breakdown is the nature of the link or links between the first enterprise and the others. This link can be financial, i.e. the enterprise may be a subsidiary : a financial group. In this case, its relations with other enterprises would obviously vary depending on whether they concerned other enterprises in the group or independent enterprises - whether or not these belonged to industry. The link can also be technical and economic, of the input/output variety, i.e. there are contacts between the first enterprise and the other(s) via a market on which there is a given

power relationship. Although the State has been taken as the starting point of the repercussions in the above examples, it can also -
sometimes at the same time - be one of the culminating points. In
fact, by means of transfers from the State to industry and vice-
versa, the State can both benefit from and contribute to the creation
of "wealth" in firms.

Part I

PROMOTION OF PRODUCTIVE INVESTMENT
OF CAPACITY INCREASES AND OF THE
INTRODUCTION OF NEW PRODUCTS AND PROCESSES

Chapter 2

THE PROMOTION OF PRODUCTIVE INVESTMENT

A. INTRODUCTION

Increased potential for economic growth depends very largely on the development and renewal of industrial production capacity. In a quantitative approach to industrial production, investment in technical assets is decisive, and it is for this reason that the public authorities have traditionally been concerned with increasing the volume of investment in industry. On top of the need to increase technical assets came other considerations relating to the distribution of the overall volume and the type of asset in question. In addition to the concern regarding regional distribution, which is only mentioned here in passing, some thought is given to sectoral distribution and, increasingly, to employment, technology and the environment. More recently, such considerations have been extended to savings in energy and raw materials.

Essentially, there are four types of investment depending on the ultimate objective:

a) extension or expansion;
b) replacement;
c) rationalisation or adaptation and, lastly,
d) cyclical growth.

Although this report is concerned mainly with the first three types of investment, the last one must also be considered in that it is not without effect from the structural angle. Moreover, the four types are not mutually exclusive. Investment for expansion, for example, is often linked with the other three, and vice-versa. However, they are not governed by the same determining factors in that some can stem from increased demand (a) and (d) and others from increased competition (c).

It is obvious from what has been said that investment is not necessarily equivalent to creating production capacity. In fact, type (a) is the only one which ought to be effective in this respect. A very large proportion of productive investment is used solely to preserve and maintain installed capacity. In the same way, the different types of investment are not equally effective in creating new jobs. Thus, type (a) normally, but not necessarily, creates new jobs at a fixed rate per unit of increased production, bearing in mind the technological component which is almost bound to be contained in investment of this sort. Type (b) should result in a fall in the number of jobs since increased productivity is often the main motive. Type (c) should very definitely cut down on jobs, while type (d) does not lead to renewed recruiting straightaway, and still less to the creation of new jobs.

The other major objective - the introduction of new products or processes - can be considered in relation to the four types of investment. The introduction of new products can be accompanied by the continuation of existing products or their replacement or modification, and the contribution to employment must be looked at from this angle. Under the present circumstances as regards the relative cost of capital and of manpower, and bearing in mind profitability prospects, the introduction of new processes usually means a fall in the number of jobs.

B. VOLUME, COMPOSITION AND USES OF INVESTMENT

As a background to this part of the report on the promoting of investment, it was thought that it would be useful to provide a brief analysis of the salient factors in the areas listed in the above title.

Among the countries in the survey, the rate of gross capital formation, i.e. the proportion of gross capital formation in GDP(1) during the period 1970-1974 (see Table V) varied in the ratio of 2 to 1, depending on the country, from Japan with an average rate of the order of 39 per cent to the United Kingdom with approximately 19 per cent. There is a leading group with Japan and then Finland and Norway (approximately 31 per cent each), followed by most of the other countries (with rates varying between 27 per cent in Germany to about 23 per cent in Sweden) and then Portugal and the United Kingdom, which has already been mentioned, further behind. With regard to the trend over the period, all the countries experienced a marked recovery of the investment rate in 1973, with the exception of Germany and Sweden, and this was despite the fact that the development of GDP was less obvious - 1973 growth rates exceeding those of 1972 in only about half the countries considered. In 1974, with GDP growth being markedly slower in most countries and negative in Greece and Japan, the share of gross capital formation declined only in half of the countries considered. In some cases the stock movement could be an explaining factor.

1) Gross Domestic Product.

TABLE V

GROWTH OF GROSS DOMESTIC PRODUCT AND RATE OF GROSS CAPITAL FORMATION FROM 1970 – 1974 IN CERTAIN MEMBER COUNTRIES

Country	Gross Domestic Product(1) Annual rate of change by volume					Gross capital formation(1) Gross domestic product(1)				
	1970	1971	1972	1973	1974	1970	1971	1972	1973	1974
Australia	5.2	5.3	3.0	6.4	1.3	27.7	25.9	24.1	27.4	25.6
Belgium	6.3	4.1	5.7	6.3	3.9	24.0	22.6	21.6	22.7	23.6
Canada	2.6	5.9	5.8	6.9	2.8	21.0	21.6	22.0	23.2	25.0
Denmark	2.7	3.4	4.6	3.3	0.5	22.8	21.5	21.4	24.1	22.4
Finland	8.3	2.4	7.0	6.5	4.2	33.0	32.5	29.3	30.7	33.6
France	5.9	5.4	5.6	5.6	3.9	26.6	25.9	26.5	27.2	26.5
Germany	5.9	2.9	3.4	5.1	0.6	28.6	27.5	27.2	26.6	23.4
Greece	7.9	7.0	8.7	7.2	-3.1	28.1	27.9	28.1	32.2	23.8
Italy	5.0	1.6	3.1	6.3	3.4	23.1	20.9	20.4	22.2	21.5
Japan	10.9	7.3	8.9	9.8	-0.9	39.3	37.9	38.2	40.6	37.6
New Zealand	3.7	2.5	4.3	6.4	2.2	27.1(3)	25.6(3)	21.6(3)	26.8(3)	36.3(3)
Norway	3.5	4.6	4.9	4.1	3.7	30.9	32.9	28.1	31.1	33.2
Portugal	7.9	5.8	8.7	7.6	2.0	17.4	19.1	20.2	20.4	19.4(2)
Spain	6.0	4.3	9.6	7.4	5.0	25.0	23.7	25.2	26.6	26.9
Sweden	5.0	0.7	2.6	3.5	4.2	25.1	22.7	22.5	21.6	23.8
United Kingdom	2.2	2.5	2.6	5.5	0.8	19.5	18.6	18.4	19.6	18.4

(1) 1970 prices
(2) GFCF
(3) At current prices

Source: National Accounts of OECD Countries 1974, Vol.II. Detailed tables, OECD, 1976.
. decimal point

TABLE VI

GROSS FIXED CAPITAL FORMATION (GFCF) IN MANUFACTURING INDUSTRY AND IN BRANCHES OF TRADING ACTIVITIES
(AS A PERCENTAGE OF TOTAL GFCF)
FROM 1970 TO 1974 IN CERTAIN MEMBER COUNTRIES

In per cent(2)

Country	Manufacturing Industry					Total Industries				
	1970	1971	1972	1973	1974	1970	1971	1972	1973	1974
Australia	13.7	13.3	11.0	..	..	84.3	84.2	83.2	83.6	80.9
Belgium	25.6	25.2	22.1	21.4	22.8	86.3	83.7	83.4	86.3	87.6
Canada	17.1	14.0	12.5	13.0	14.5	82.4	81.6	82.4	84.0	83.7
Denmark	11.6	10.7	9.6	10.1	..	97.2	97.4	97.5	98.2	..
Finland	24.0(3)	24.6(3)	22.5(3)	20.7(3)	23.2	83.0	83.5	81.8	83.6	85.1
France	33.1(3)	33.2(3)	32.6(3)	30.4(3)	30.8(3)	95.8	96.2	96.7	96.9	97.1
Germany	..	..	..	..	..	98.8	99.0	99.2	99.3	99.4
Greece	14.2	14.9	15.9	15.4	20.6	91.4	91.4	92.1	93.6	..
Italy	30.5(1)	33.0(1)	32.7(1)	35.2(1)	..	76.6	73.1	72.4	74.4	..
Japan	26.1	22.8	19.1	19.3	..	..	..	..	..	..
New Zealand	..	..	..	..	..	84.0	85.1	81.5	84.5	85.4
Norway	15.2	14.1	12.7	11.4	14.8	87.6	87.6	88.9	90.9	89.5
Portugal	31.3	31.0	29.6	28.9	30.1	..	..	..	..	..
Spain	..	..	..	..	..	..	..	..	..	..
Sweden	17.4	18.0	17.6	19.4	22.1	79.4	81.0	82.0	83.9	85.0
United Kingdom	22.7	21.0	17.6	17.5	20.1	84.2	83.9	83.3	83.6	85.2

(1) Including mining and quarrying, electricity, water and gas and building and public works.
(2) Percentages calculated on the basis of data at current prices.
(3) Including mining and quarrying, electricity, gas and water.

Source: National Accounts of OECD Countries 1974, Vol.II. Detailed tables, OECD 1976.
.. Not available
. Decimal point

TABLE VII

USES OF GROSS FIXED CAPITAL FORMATION (GFCF)(1) FROM 1970 TO 1974 IN CERTAIN MEMBER COUNTRIES

In per cent(2)

	Residential buildings					Other buildings or constructions					Transport equipment and machinery and other investment goods				
	1970	1971	1972	1973	1974	1970	1971	1972	1973	1974	1970	1971	1972	1973	1974
Australia	18.7	19.4	21.8	22.6	19.3	38.2	38.0	37.4	36.2	39.5	43.1	42.6	40.7	41.2	41.2
Belgium	25.0	20.2	21.4	25.9	27.8	35.7(3	42.5(3)	41.7(3)	38.5(3)	35.7(3	39.3	37.3	36.9	35.7	36.5
Canada	19.5	21.7	23.6	24.4	23.3	45.5	45.3	42.9	40.7	41.1	34.9	32.9	33.4	34.9	35.5
Denmark	23.1	21.9	26.1	28.2	25.0	35.8(3	36.8(3)	33.4(3)	31.2(3)	33.4(3	41.5	41.5	40.3	40.5	41.4
Finland	24.4	23.9	26.0	25.5	26.0	38.5(3	37.1(3)	35.7(3)	38.0(3)	37.3(3	37.1	39.0	38.3	36.4	36.7
France	28.5	28.5	28.2	28.7	29.1	33.0(3	32.1(3)	32.5(3)	31.8(3)	31.6(3	47.7	48.7	48.7	48.5	48.4
Germany	20.5	22.0	25.1	25.7	23.5	33.7	33.1	32.3	32.1	34.2	46.8	45.8	43.5	43.1	43.6
Greece	24.5	24.6	27.4	26.9	20.5	35.8	35.1	33.5	33.1	36.5	35.6	35.9	34.8	35.7	40.1
Italy	32.7	29.4	29.8	29.3	..	30.3	30.7	29.7	27.3	..	36.9	39.9	40.5	43.4	..
Japan	20.7	20.3	22.2	24.1	23.4	79.3(4)	79.7(4)	77.8(4)	75.9(4)	76.6(4	..	..	..	..	..
New Zealand	..	..	..	..	..	..	..	..	..	..	..	..	..	..	..
Norway	18.4	17.5	19.2	17.6	16.6	36.7	34.6	38.4	40.3	45.4	44.4	47.3	41.6	41.5	37.6
Portugal	14.3	13.1	14.2	16.2	20.7	37.6	38.7	37.3	39.5	38.2	45.8	46.1	46.9	43.0	39.8
Spain	24.1	24.4	23.6	25.0	27.2	36.2(3)	37.7(3)	36.9	35.6	35.8	39.7	37.8	39.5	39.4	37.0
Sweden	25.6	25.8	25.2	24.4	20.6	40.6	38.9	39.1	37.3	36.7	32.8	34.0	34.1	36.9	41.5
United Kingdom	17.5	18.2	19.6	19.5	19.3	30.9	31.2	30.8	31.0	33.7	48.6	47.2	45.2	45.0	44.0

(1) GFCF = 100 %.

(2) Percentages calculated on the basis of data given at current prices.

(3) Including the development and improvement of crops and orchards.

(4) Total GFCF less residential buildings.

Note: The total for the rows per annum can amount to or exceed 100 per cent depending upon whether GFCF for "land improvement" and "breeding stock" is positive or negative.

Source: National Accounts of OECD Countries 1974, Vo.II. Detailed tables, OECD 1976.

.. not available

. decimal point

During the period 1970 to 1974, the proportion of manufacturing
industry in GFCF(1) (see Table VI) varied for the most part between
about 10 per cent (Denmark) to over 21 per cent (Belgium), and was
falling in almost all countries except Greece, which is a more
recently industrialised country. (The figures for France and Italy
are not comparable with those for other countries.) In 1974, manufacturing industry increased its share in GFCF in those countries
for which data are available.

Table VII shows the breakdown of total GFCF, by uses, from 1970
to 1974. From the point of view of industry, it can be seen that
expenditure in fixed capital goods and transport amounts on average
to some 41 per cent of total GFCF, with France, the United Kingdom
and Germany in the lead followed closely by Portugal. In these
three countries, the proportion is in fact on average greater than
45 per cent of total GFCF. Canada and Greece come last among the
countries considered with proportions in the region of 35 per cent.
In Spain, Norway, the United Kingdom and Portugal it is noticeable
that the proportion of residential buildings is very small, whereas
residential investment in Italy is proportionately the highest compared with the other countries. It is also apparent that investment
in capital goods and transport, i.e. which concerns production capacity, is tending to stabilise or to decrease in relation to other
investment in most of countries considered (with the exception of
Canada, Sweden and Italy). In Belgium, Denmark, Finland, Germany
and Sweden the share of these investments has increased slightly in
1974.

To conclude this brief survey, it seems necessary to stress
that although the data used are, a priori, broadly comparable, they
are nevertheless very general and should therefore be used or inter-
preted with great caution.

In what follows, we shall deal firstly with investment support
policies designed to increase production capacity and provide new
jobs, and secondly with those whose purpose it is to encourage the
introduction of new products or processes.

---

1) Gross Fixed Capital Formation.

Chapter 3

INCREASING PRODUCTION CAPACITY AND CREATING NEW JOBS

A. INTRODUCTION

In order to pursue such a traditional and important objective,
but one which is at the same time fairly general as to the way it is
formulated, the public authorities in Member countries have in the
course of time developed both fiscal and financial instruments.

The object of fiscal instruments is to influence investment via
their effect on the volume of internal financing, i.e. on the basis
of enterprises' own funds, by adjusting taxation in relation to a
given initial tax situation. There are three main sources of self-
financing: depreciation and provisions, undistributed profits and,
if need be, the proceeds from selling assets. In some cases, other
fiscal provisions can apply depending upon the tax structure in the
country in question, for example those concerning investment funds.

In the absence of an internationally accepted definition of the
concept of self-financing, an international comparison of self-
financing rates or of their trend would seem somewhat hazardous and,
on reflection, perhaps not significant. An existing rate must in
fact be considered in conjunction with the type of enterprise, its
financing structures and the profitability of investment, the national or international capital market and the structure of interest
rates on this market. The trend of the self-financing rate over
time must also be considered in conjunction with the trend of the
above-mentioned factors. Perhaps even more important is an investigation of the part played by self-financing in the development of
industrial structures and its advantages and disadvantages, leading
eventually to a study of the policies pursued by the public authorities.

Self-financing is generally recognised as having a certain
number of disadvantages which can, essentially speaking, be summarised as follows:

a) prolongation;
b) resistance to change and, lastly;
c) a cyclical effect.

a) Self-financing can in fact have the effect of prolonging existing structures, which is not necessarily undesirable at enterprise level, but can become so should it run counter to governmental objectives involving greater mobility of capital, as for example with regional policy or structural policy.

b) Resistance to change may be encountered in declining sectors where demand is falling and profit margins are consequently smaller. If priority is given to self-financing, particularly in small enterprises, this may have the effect of delaying decisions to invest in structural adaptation, rationalisation or modernisation.

c) The cyclical effect implies that there is a necessary link between the self-financing level and the decision to invest, and it can cause an increase in investment during a boom period which may be contrary to the objectives of cyclical policy.

On the other hand, self-financing does undoubtedly have a certain number of advantages as regards:

a) cost;
b) volume; and
c) negotiation.

a) Self-financed capital is not burdened by the cost of bank commissions in particular, administrative complications and, above all, taxation - in the case of profit distribution especially.

b) There are no "flights" of self-financed capital on the capital market, i.e. there is no reduction in volume.

c) Self-financing in many ways constitutes a part of the firm's independence and an argument in negotiations with lenders, i.e. it is a precondition for borrowing. Self-financing is therefore a relatively inexpensive form of financing, and provision for it should not therefore be discouraged.

B. FISCAL INSTRUMENTS

Depreciation mechanisms

Depreciation, which is an ambiguous concept, has two main facets: one fiscal and the other economic. From the fiscal point of view, depreciation is looked upon as a non-taxable cost and is shown, for a given fiscal period, as the writing off of that part of the price of a fixed asset corresponding to the loss of value of the said asset through use. From the economic standpoint, this observation is valid during periods of zero growth and low inflation, but is less so during periods of rapid growth. In this case, depreciation is one of the best ways of financing the growth of an enterprise; it is this conception which largely prevails nowadays.

33

Tax provisions in this connection should in principle prescribe depreciation over a period of much the same duration as for accounting or economic purposes. The incentive to invest stems from the acceleration of fiscal depreciation in relation to accounting. This margin of incentive varies according, first of all, to the degree of acceleration of fiscal depreciation and, secondly, to the changes in duration of depreciation for accounting purposes. Some countries' legislation allows enterprises to declare accounting depreciation rates which differ from and are lower than fiscal depreciation rates. This possibility enables joint stock companies, for example, to show shareholders lower accounting depreciation in order to show higher profits.

The accelerated depreciation mechanism differs from the subsidy mainly by virtue of the fact that it constitutes the deferral of part of an enterprise's fiscal liabilities rather than their abolition, in that the corollary of an initial acceleration, i.e. an increase in the initial instalments, is a reduction of the following instalments with their effect on the basis of assessment of tax on profits. The degree of acceleration can be measured by comparison with a traditional method of depreciation, i.e. the linear technique.

Depreciation concerns all the different types of assets, building and plant in particular as well as non-material assets, and can be varied according to the type of asset, the type of proprietor enterprise and the sector or region considered. The value of the assets to be written off is usually a function of the original cost which may constitute the ceiling. If a higher depreciation allowance is being considered, it can either be recognised that the total depreciation exceeds the original cost, or the original cost can be upvalued.

The acceleration is itself an incentive to invest in that, from the fiscal standpoint (depreciation being looked upon as a cost) it magnifies the consequences of an accelerated rate of investment. Conversely, if the rate of investment slows, fiscal depreciation will be reduced. As a result, the public authorities in countries where investment is tending to slacken will be tempted to provide an additional incentive by gradually allowing depreciation rates to accelerate.

As a policy instrument, however, legislation regarding depreciation soon comes up against certain limitations. In the first place, there is an absolute limitation in cases where complete freedom is allowed regarding depreciation. Secondly, despite the many changes in legislation made by certain authorities (discrimination according to the type of fixed asset, the region or sector in which the activity takes place, for example), the general effect of this instrument can be to preserve structures and encourage excess capital expenditure

in certain branches. Thirdly, the funds left in the hands of enterprises, and exempt from taxation, may not be used in the ways recommended by the public authorities. In some cases, therefore, legis-
lators have been careful to introduce observation mechanisms. Lastly,
the possible advantages of accelerated depreciation as regards self-
financing can only be used if the enterprise does in fact make a
profit. In view of the fluctuations that can occur as regards the
existence and level of enterprises' profits from one year to the
next, changes have been made in some cases which enable enterprises
either to relate depreciation to an earlier year or, if this is not
possible, to spread the losses over a period of time.

Measuring the impact

Legislation concerning depreciation is part of a whole set of
measures comprising all taxation relating to enterprises. Several
components of this taxation can affect the cost of capital for the
entrepreneur and, consequently, his investment decision and choice.
The main aspects are fiscal depreciation, company tax, and tax
credits to the extent that they concern investment or subsidies.
Other components are indirect taxes payable on purchase of capital
goods (excluding VAT), land tax or systems of tax deferment such as
investment reserves which are established free of taxation. The
fiscal cost of capital is difficult to define in that an asset provides a certain number of services during its life, the cost of
which must be divided into portions corresponding to accounting
periods. This cost can therefore be defined as the acquisition cost
of the asset (depreciable) and the cost of the capital needed for its
acquisition (in terms of anticipated income or of paid interest) adjusted in relation to variations in the market price of the assets
over time.

Theoretical studies have been carried out with the object of
determining the cost of capital depending on the main fiscal components listed above. Their impact can be demonstrated by means of
a simple example(1). The following data: price of plant: 100, depreciation period: 8 years, discount rate 10 per cent, give a minimum annual cost of capital of 18.74, in the absence of company tax.
Introduction of a company tax of 50 per cent, cost: 37.48. Reduction of the depreciation period to 4 years, cost: 22.64. Tax credit
of 5 per cent, cost: 20.76. If the rate of the company tax was
only 10 per cent, the cost would be reduced to 19.44. Taxation has
no effect when the cost of the asset is deducted immediately from
the company tax. This example demonstrates the complexity of fiscal
influences on the cost of capital for entrepreneurs.

1) Using the formulae established in: Fromm C. (Ed.), Tax Incentives
   and Capital Spending, Brookings, 1971.

Some country notes

On the basis of the information available, the following observations can be made concerning certain specific countries.

In Belgium, for example, the Act of 30th December, 1970 on economic growth enables the State, bearing in mind regional or sectoral considerations and in the case of operations consistent with the general economic interest, to extend fiscal advantages to specific enterprises by allowing them to write off annual amounts equal to double the linear depreciation for a period of three years. Other legal stipulations provide for tax exemption inter alia on capital gains or real estate (called "précompte immobilier").

In Canada, certain company taxation measures were adopted in August 1973. The object of these measures was to improve the international competitiveness of Canada's manufacturing and processing firms. They concerned company taxation and fiscal depreciation in particular, and consisted of reducing the rate on income from 50 per cent in 1972 to 46 per cent in 1976 and in subsequent years. To the same end and at the same time, the Canadian Government introduced an immediate reduction down to 40 per cent in the rate of company tax applicable to profits obtained in Canada on the basis of manufacturing and processing activities, and rapid depreciation over two years for capital goods intended for the same activities. These measures have been extended indefinitely. A special effort has been made in this country to determine the effect of these measures. A survey was undertaken of a scientific sample of enterprises, and this was supplemented by interviews in 25 per cent of the enterprises consulted which had answered the written survey. The aim was to obtain information on the effect of the measure in the following areas: the enterprise's investment, employment and sales plans, its price policy and its competitiveness in national and foreign markets. The interim report drawn up as a result of the survey can be summarised as follows: fiscal measures were expected to have a significant and continuous effect by improving the competitive situation of processing industries and by increasing the capacity of these enterprises to develop investment and sales and to supply a growing number of jobs for Canada's labour force. A final report on this question was to be submitted at the end of 1974.

In Spain, under the legal provisions dating from 1960 and reframed in 1967, accelerated depreciation is considered to include not only normal depreciation for the writing-down or loss of value of assets, and subject to prior government approval, but also depreciation which is part of a special or accelerated plan. In the latter case, the annual coefficients applied could not, except in special cases, exceed 40 per cent of the value of the asset as shown on the balance sheet. The main object of the system was to encourage

self-financing by enterprises. Up until 1971, this type of depreciation remained almost constantly at a level of five per cent of total
depreciation. In 1971, however, the proportion suddenly increased
to 15 per cent.

Finland provides an example of regional application of the system of accelerated depreciation. Under the 1969 Act on tax reliefs
to promote productive activity in developing areas, tax advantages
are applicable to industrial enterprises which increase production
capacity and create new jobs in these regions. These provisions
allow firms to write-down over 10 years and at whatever rate they
choose material assets acquired between 1960 and 1970 and installed
in one of the development areas. A further initial allowance of 3
per cent of expenditure on new assets is authorised on the tax revenue
of enterprises in the least developed of the two regions. In addition to this measure, enterprises in development areas can be exempted
from presumptive taxation by local authorities for the period during
which they receive other regional tax allowances. Nor do they pay
land tax or stamp duty. New regional legislation was to have been
introduced in 1975 on the expiry of the 1969 Act. Because of the
overlapping of the various fiscal provisions described above, it is
impossible to measure the impact either of all or of the most important of them - i.e. that concerning accelerated depreciation.

In France, industrial enterprises carrying out operations coming
under regional development policy may benefit, in addition to temporary exemption from the business licence tax and reduction of the
transfer duty (see paragraph 90 hereafter), from an exceptional
writing down of 25 per cent of the cost of new construction meeting
siting requirements. The exceptional write-down must take place immediately after construction is completed. The residual value may
be written down over the normal depreciation period. Authorisations
issued covered Fr.493 million of new construction in 1974, and the
discounted cost may be put at 10 per cent of the total amount.

In Greece, the measures relating to accelerated depreciation
introduced on 1st January, 1973 had two objectives: to decentralise
Greek industry and thus use industrialisation to promote regional development; secondly, to make better use of existing fixed assets by
employing one or more teams of workers. This measure, which applied
to all industrial and craft enterprises, can be varied according to
the region in which the enterprise is located and the number of teams.
The basic rate can in this way be raised from 25 to 200 per cent.

In Italy, it is planned to encourage the creation of production
capacity by allowing anticipated depreciation in the personal income
tax code.

In Japan, a measure was introduced in 1952 with the object of
promoting the modernisation and rationalisation of important industries by introducing a special depreciation rate for certain capital

goods. The rate was originally 50 per cent for the first year (in addition to normal depreciation); this was lowered in 1961 and 1966 down to 25 per cent, and was to be abolished by 31st March, 1976.

In the United Kingdom, as the outcome of the various legislative changes made in this area - mainly through four Acts: the Capital Allowance Act 1968 and the three Finance Acts of 1970, 1971 and 1972, regional policy finally took precedence over the sectoral approach. With the system becoming increasingly complex, the need to simplify it led the United Kingdom authorities to align the rates. Preferential treatment for particular regions or sectors became pointless. The description will make it easier to follow the course of events (see Table 1).

Special investment allowances

The object of special investment allowances is usually to give enterprises an extra incentive to invest by reducing the cost of investment and also, by making the advantages available for a limited time only, to concentrate orders and thereby give a boost to the cyclical situation by means of investment. The degree of stimulation varies depending on whether the presumptive allowance can be made as part of the depreciable value of the asset or is additional to this value. In the second instance, the allowance can be considered to be an implicit revaluation of this value. The allowance can sometimes be varied according to the region or the type of investment. It may be granted automatically or, on the contrary, it may have to be agreed by the tax authorities.

Australia has in the past used tax allowances for investment in order to encourage the growth of industrial investment. The allowance was first introduced in 1962 during a downturn in economic activity, and remained in force until it was stopped in 1971. After being reintroduced a year later in order to stimulate investment, it was stopped again in August 1973. This allowance provided for a reduction of the tax base equivalent to 20 per cent of investment in certain factories and plant, and was in addition to normal depreciation. It can be estimated that the loss in tax revenue amounted to 45 million Australian dollars in 1972/1973 and 54 million Australian dollars in 1973/1974.

In Greece too, in order to encourage investment and regional development, industrial and craft enterprises proceeding with new investment can deduct from their net profits a percentage of between 50 and 100 per cent of their capital expenditure, depending on the location of the investment. The 50 per cent rate applies to investment carried out between 1st January, 1973 and 31st December, 1977, and the 100 per cent rate to investment between 1st January, 1973 and 31st December, 1982. To encourage the creation of working capital, a further 10 or 20 per cent of the value of the investment may be deducted.

38

TREND OF TAX LEGISLATION IN REGARD TO DEPRECIATION FROM THE 1968 CAPITAL ALLOWANCES ACT TO THE 1972 FINANCE ACT

Type of asset	Initial deduction		Initial deduction for depreciation
A. 1968 ACT			
i) Buildings for industrial use(1)	15% of the construction cost(2)		4% of the cost(3)(4)
ii) Capital goods(1)(5)	30%(6)(7)(2)		A. 15% B. 6.25%
			A. 20% B. 8.50%
			A. 25% B. 11.25%
			(8)(3)
iii) Mining activities	40%(7)		
iv) Scientific research	100%(2)		
B. 1970 ACT	Assisted regions	Others	
Buildings for industrial use(10)	40%(18)	30%	No change
C. 1971 ACT			
Capital goods(11)(5)	100%(12)(6)(14) (2)(18) 60%(13)(6)	60%	25% diminishing balance(19)
Mining activities	100%(11)(18) (2)		
D. 1972 ACT			
Buildings for industrial use	40%		
Capital goods	(15) 100%(16) 80%(13) (18)	80%	
	100%(17)(6)		

(1) Total deductions must not exceed the cost.
(2) Authorised for the year in which the expenditure occurred.
(3) Authorised for each year of use.
(4) 2% if expenditure occurred before 6.11.72.
(5) Ships may be written off as the owner likes.
(6) Does not normally apply to motor vehicles.
(7) Does not normally apply if a cash investment grant has been made.
(8) Rates A or B apply depending on the method of depreciation adopted: A diminishing balance; A. diminishing balance; B. Straight-line and the length of useful life.
(9) At rates depending upon the foreseeable life span of the mine or at 5% diminishing balance.
(10) Applies to expenditure incurred between 6.4.1970 and 5.4.1972.
(11) Applies to expenditure incurred after 26.10.1970.
(12) Applies to immobile capital goods for industrial purposes
(13) Applies to other capital goods.
(14) If the depreciation capacity is exceeded, the surplus can be carried back to the previous three years.
(15) Applies to expenditure incurred between 19.7.1971 and 22.3.1972 and made known in July 1971.
(16) Applies to fixed capital goods irrespective of their use.
(17) Applies to expenditure incurred after 21.3.1972.
(18) Also applies in Northern Ireland.
(19) Authorised for each year of use except for the year for which the initial deduction is authorised.

The "fiscal aid to investment" introduced in <u>Spain</u> in 1971, renewed in 1973 and supplemented in January 1975, has as its basic objective to give support for those industrial sectors in need of rapid expansion. It goes hand in hand with the measure providing for repayment of the general turnover tax to those companies which acquire certain items of capital equipment. The Decree provides for the deduction from the fiscal licence fee and from company tax assessments, in the form of an investment allowance, of a sum equal to 7 per cent of investment actually made. The sectors which will benefit are the following:

1. food industry;
2. pulp and paper manufacture;
3. agricultural chemical industries and their raw materials;
4. leather;
5. construction;
6. cement industry;
7. copper, iron, tin, zinc, lead, potash and pyrite mines;
8. motor-vehicle and auxiliary industries; and
9. machine tools.

In April 1975 in the framework of economic policy measures, a special scheme of fiscal support for productive investment has been introduced. It exempts from the general tax on corporate income 10 per cent of that part of investment which exceeds 7 per cent of fiscal capital, and this will be deducted from the provisional surcharge of the tax in question.

In November 1975 the Government granted a discharge of obligations contracted to carry out investment under the investment provision scheme or the export investment reserve scheme.

The system introduced in 1963 by which specific industrial sectors can be declared of "preferential interest" constitutes an example of a sectorally differentiated application of essentially tax advantages. The benefits enjoyed by sectors declared to be of preferential interest are as follows: (1) compulsory expropriation of land required for their establishment or enlargement, (2) reduction, which may reach 95 per cent, of the following taxes: issue of stocks and shares, taxes and stamp duties on instruments of incorporation or for increasing the capital of companies concerned, tax on outlays for the acquisition of capital equipment and tools during the period of installation, protective customs duties and other taxes imposed on the import of capital equipment and tools where these are not manufactured in Spain. Free depreciation over the first five years. The following have been declared of preferential interest, set out in chronological order:

Chemical monomers and polymers	23rd Dec. 1971
Nuclear steam generating systems	23rd Dec. 1972
Private cars	23rd Dec. 1972
Sulphuric acid and phosphoric acid derived from domestically produced pyrites	5th April, 1973
Compounds, parts and equipment for motor vehicles	28th Feb. 1974
Steel-making complexes	14th March, 1974
Electronic apparatus and equipment and their components	20th July, 1974
Food industries	14th Nov. 1974

For similiar cyclical purposes, the special 10 per cent investment allowance introduced in <u>Sweden</u> at the beginning of 1971 concerned
all private and corporate bodies and applied to certain investments
in the course of that year. The allowance was not granted automatically, and had to be claimed by the taxpayer.

Investment reserves

On the pattern of the Swedish investment reserve set up in 1938,
some other countries have introduced investment reserve systems
(Spain, Denmark, Finland for example). The principle of these systems is generally as follows: firms are entitled to set aside, free
of tax, a specific proportion of their taxable profits which are
placed partly with a financial institution, often the central bank,
in order to help finance investment at a later date - possibly with
the assistance of the public authorities. Two observations should
be made in this connection: the time when the funds placed in reserve become available will be decided(1) outside the enterprise but
in consultation with it, and the objectives pursued in releasing
funds may be broader than cyclical policy; they may be sectoral or
regional, or even more qualitative - e.g. the protection of the environment. The success of this type of system depends very largely
on the time when the authorisation is given, the period of application and, consequently, the choice of prior indicators.

In view of the far-reaching effect that economic fluctuations
can have on enterprises and industrial structures, it may be worthwhile considering briefly the effects that investment funds can have.
These effects may be considered firstly at the time when the investment fund is credited, and again when it is debited.

When the enterprise sets aside the authorised part of its taxable profits (the system relies therefore on there being a profit),
its cash reserves may be increased to the extent that the portion

1) These authorisations can be in the form of an obligation enjoining
the enterprise to use the funds, or of an authorisation extended
to enterprises making a withdrawal claim.

which has to be deposited with a financial institution is lower than
the rate of the tax on profits payable if the investment fund is not
drawn on. The resulting benefit may be looked upon as an anticipated
depreciation of capital invested with assistance from the fund at a
later date inasmuch as this capital can no longer be written-down
after the effective purchase of capital goods.

This improved liquidity situation is the initial incentive.
However, this benefit is not necessarily decisive in persuading the
entrepreneur to proceed with deposits. He will weigh it against investment opportunities which may arise in the short term in that the
anticipated profitability rate may exceed the incentive deriving from
the use of the reserves.

Assuming that the entrepreneur makes the deposit, the improved
liquidity situation can have a destablizing effect when economic
activity is at a high level. It is probable, though, that the firm's
investment plans will be favourably influenced (tending towards stability) by knowledge of the advantageous conditions which will probably be available during a recession.

When there is a general authorisation to draw on investment resources, the stabilizing effect is equal to the amount of investment
over and above that which would have taken place anyway if the reserves had not been drawn on. This margin is obviously difficult to
determine, but apart from this effect of shifting investment over
time, can reserves prompt firms to develop their long-term investment
plans? Sweden's experience does not seem to offer a precise answer.
It should, however, be said that the prime objective of this instrument is to stabilize economic activity in the short-term.

Set up in 1938, Sweden's investment reserve did not become a
major factor in that country's economic policy until 1955. The reserve is first and foremost a cyclical regulator whose primary objective is to safeguard employment in periods of crisis. On the principle that investment can generate additional employment, the reserve is used to promote productive investment. Even so, it has
been used for other purposes such as the implementation of regional
or structural policy.

In practice, there are two types of reserve: the General
Reserve and the Forestry Reserve. The latter is of relatively limited
scope compared with the former, as is shown in Table 2.

The mechanism of these reserves is as follows: companies may
set aside up to 40 per cent of their profits free of tax, as an investment reserve. Part of this 46 per cent (in some cases, 40 per
cent), is deposited with the Central Bank but earns no interest. In
a period of recession as defined by the Government, the reserve may
be drawn on to finance specified types of investment, and its use
be coupled with a deduction from taxable profits equivalent to 10 per
cent of the capital thus employed.

Table 2

SWEDEN

INVESTMENT RESERVES HELD AT THE SWEDISH NATIONAL BANK

(Kr. million at current prices)

	1966	1967	1968	1969	1970	1971	1972
General investment reserves							
Deposits	299	289	420	440	503	403	453
Withdrawals	165	570	525	251	330	595	466
Balance at end of year	1,263	982	877	1,065	1,238	1,045	1,033
Forestry investment reserves							
Deposits	5	–	4	4	4	3	11
Withdrawals	2	6	5	1	–	10	2
Balance at end of year	13	7	5	8	12	5	14

Source: Sveriges Riksbank.

This gives the public authorities an effective anti-cyclical instrument. During upswings, it is in a company's interest to feed its investment reserves since this reduces the tax bill. In less buoyant periods it has a source of cash readily available. Decisions to authorise the release of funds from these reserves are taken by the Labour Board acting on behalf of the Government or by the Government itself. To avail themselves of a release of funds, companies have to comply with Government directives, particularly in the case of special releases. These are authorised for very specific purposes such as regional or sectoral policy. The following two examples illustrate this.

In 1966, a special release was authorised for 10 firms located in development areas and for 65 textile firms in the County of Älvsborg. These reserves – Kr.280 million provided funds for about 75 per cent of the total capital investment involved (Kr.377 million).

On 19th May, 1972 a special Government release was made to firms in the mining and manufacturing industries to purchase buildings, on condition that they did so by the end of April, 1973. In the debelopment areas, the opportunity applied to all investment schemes in these industries without any time limit. On 29th August, 1972, the arrangements were extended to all branches of industry.

As is shown in Table 3, withdrawals from the investment reserves have allowed a far from negligible proportion of investment to be financed, particularly when economic activity was at a low level.

Table 3

SWEDEN

ASSISTED INVESTMENT AND TOTAL PRODUCTIVE INVESTMENT

(Kr. million at current prices)

	1966	1967-1968	1969	1970	1971	1972
Assisted investment (excluding stocks)	377	3,385	1,163	1,782	1,614	1,038
Gross private fixed capital formation (excluding residential building)	12,807	25,511	12,966	14,580	15,573	17,428
Percentage	2.9	13.3	9.0	12.2	10.4	6.0

Sources: National Labour Market Office, Central Statistics Bureau and the National Institute for Economic Research.

Note: Assisted investment has been broken down over time in accordance with the date of authorisation.

Apart from this general impact, it seemed worthwhile consider-ing the sectoral structure of the estimated cost of investment fi-nanced with the help of either general or special withdrawals from investment reserves. The following two tables give a very clear indication of the cumulative effect of withdrawals on the metal working and machinery industry and, consequently, its predominant share in total manufacturing industry. In the first place, any in-vestment in this very capital-intensive industry will result in rela-tively substantial expenditure, but doubtless this is not specific to this industry; secondly, its own investment expenditure is a function of demand for capital goods, to which must be added demand for capital goods in other industries proceeding with investment[1].

In Finland, the public authorities instituted several invest-ment reserves, starting in 1954. Their mechanism and purpose are very much the same as those of the investment reserves in Sweden. In accordance with the basic regulations of the General Investment Reserve set up in 1955, an industrial enterprise (in Sweden the sys-tem applies to all enterprises irrespective of the branch of indus-try) can transfer to an investment reserve up to 30 per cent of its annual profits (in Sweden the basic rate is 46 per cent). This rate can however be increased by the Government if warranted by special circumstances. In fact, the percentage has varied between 30 and 80 per cent. Use of the reserves to finance investment is subject

1) For further information on the Swedish system, see: "Investment Funds", by Rugberg and Ohman, Occasional Paper 5, National Institute of Economic Research, Stockholm, 1971.

TABLE 4

SWEDEN

SECTORAL BREAKDOWN OF THE ESTIMATED COST OF INVESTMENT FINANCED BY MEANS OF

GENERAL WITHDRAWALS FROM THE INVESTMENT RESERVES

FROM 19th MAY, 1967 TO 31st DECEMBER, 1968

Kr. million at current prices

Sector of activity	19.5.67 to 30.4.68	2.5.68 to 31.12.68	TOTAL	%
Primary sector	79	56	135	-
Secondary sector	1,652	661	2,313	100
Metalworking and machinery	785	352	1,137	49.2
Non-metallic minerals	87	23	110	4.8
Wood products	75	34	109	4.7
Pulp and paper	164	40	204	8.8
Printing	46	18	64	2.8
Food products	111	30	141	6.1
Beverages and tobacco	117	71	188	8.1
Textiles and clothing	92	27	119	5.1
Leather goods, hides and rubber	16	4	20	0.9
Chemicals	159	62	221	9.6
Other activities	118	127	245	-
TOTAL	1,850	844	2,694	-

Source: National Labour Market Office

TABLE 5

SWEDEN

SECTORAL BREAKDOWN OF THE COST OF INVESTMENT FINANCED BY MEANS OF

SPECIAL WITHDRAWALS FROM THE INVESTMENT RESERVES

FROM 1969 TO 1972

Kr. million at current prices

Sector of activity	1969	1970	1971	1972	TOTAL	%
Primary sector	114	3	40	48	205	-
Manufacturing Industry	911	1,412	1,171	660	4,154	100
Food, beverages and tobacco	2	5	90	68	165	4.0
Textiles, clothing and leather	3	27	41	41	112	2.7
Wood products	9	3	75	39	126	3.0
Pulp and paper, printing	46	32	106	178	362	8.7
Chemicals, rubber and plastics	57	23	108	111	299	7.2
Non-metallic minerals	2	1	31	11	45	1.1
Steel and metalworking	8	544	24	12	588	14.2
Machinery	784	777	690	197	2,448	58.9
Miscellaneous	-	-	6	3	9	0.2
Tertiary sector	138	367	402	329	1,236	-
TOTAL	1,163	1,782	1,614	1,038	5,597	-

Source: National Labour Market Office.

to authorisation or instruction by the Government. These reserves
are exempt from property tax;   likewise, they can be deducted from
the company's taxable income on condition that the sum corresponding
to the income tax is deposited with the Central Bank. These deposits
bear tax-free interest. In the majority of cases, these tax allowances are only of temporary benefit to the enterprise in that it
cannot write-down those assets financed out of the investment reserves. The latter can be used for the purchase of capital goods
(buildings, machinery and plant) and also for the development of
vocational training and the application of pollution control measures.
As an indication of the trend of investment reserves, it is worth
noting that in 1970, for example, a total of Mks.5 million was put
to reserve, i.e. 1.3 per cent of all industrial profits. At the
same time, total deposits with the Central Bank amounted to Mks.64
million (i.e. the total budgetary loss of revenue), reserves totalling Mks.130 million. For the same year, industrial investment
amounted to approximately Mks.4,000 million. Investment reserves
were exhausted in 1973 and then partially reconstituted, amounting to
Mks.73 million at the end of 1974, while deposits with the Central
Bank reached Mks.31 million. At that time, these deposits were equal
to between 38 and 43 per cent of total investment reserves.

This system is above all an instrument for regulating the cyclical situation, and in this respect it can be said with some certainty
that it has had positive results as regards both investment and employment. It would seem more difficult, on the other hand, to determine the system's long-term effects, i.e. to what extent it has
helped to procure investment which would otherwise have remained a
dead letter.

Apart from this system which is of fairly general application,
other mechanisms have been introduced which are of more limited scope
as regards either the type of activity eligible or the sort of investment which can benefit. Thus, 1954 saw the introduction of the
system for the wood products industry and 1964 the system for the
mining industry - which lasted until 1976. In 1966, an export reserve system was set up, while 1969 saw the institution of a system
for developing economic growth and the protection of the environment.

In Japan, measures introduced in 1964 and - after an initial
period of 3 years - renewed since, provide for the establishment of
a reserve fund for developing investment abroad, including the ex-
ploitation of raw materials. This fund can be supplied free of tax
from the partial counterpart of the cost of acquiring investments
abroad and the losses incurred. Since the system was extended in
1971 to cover all investment abroad, the annual loss to tax revenue
has varied between Yen 14 to 15 billion.

Particularly in view of the fact that traditional tax measures (for example accelerated depreciation) often only benefit enterprises making profits, Germany introduced in 1969 an investment grant system which was considered fiscal since it was decided by the tax authorities and financed from the proceeds of income tax and company tax. For the creation, conversion or basic rationalisation of an establishment located in a specified region, a taxpayer may ask for a grant equivalent (since February 19, 1973) to 7.5 per cent of the cost on condition that the operation meets a double criterion concerning the national economic interest and the principles and objectives of town and regional planning. The main reason for introducing this system was the need to create and preserve permanent and new jobs. The authorities' loss in tax revenue over the 5 years 1971 to 1975 totalled DM.2,204 million. Given the rates applied, it can be calculated that subsidised investment probably totalled between DM.22 and 25 billion.

Table 6 shows the position of this instrument compared with all the other measures designed to assist investment in specified regions - particularly the eastern border.

Table 6

GERMANY

COMPARISON BETWEEN FISCAL AND FINANCIAL INSTRUMENTS
DESIGNED TO PROMOTE INVESTMENT IN ASSISTED REGIONS

(DM million)

	1971	1972	1973	1974	1975
Fiscal instruments (accelerated depreciation, 1971) (1)	290	320	390	480	556
Financial instruments:					
Investment grants, 1969 (1)	486	665	664	800	579
Investment subsidies, 1969	532	532	532	532	588
Loan guarantees, 1969 (2)	400	400	400	400	400
Total:	1,708	1,917	1,986	2,212	2,123

1) Loss in tax revenue.
2) Annual ceiling on guarantees.

According to the authorities, this system of investment grants has proved a very effective method of promoting investment in the assisted regions.

Other fiscal measures

Apart from fiscal measures found in a great many countries, of which the main ones have been discussed above, there are certain

national particularities depending both on the type of problem under
consideration (excessive splitting up of investment) and the specific
features of the national tax system. In <u>Belgium</u>, there is exemption
for a maximum of five years from the advance payment of tax (précompte immobilier) in respect of real estate investment which has
attracted aids as laid down by law; in <u>Greece</u>, investment projects
exceeding a certain size are exempt from various taxes; in <u>France</u>,
industrial enterprises carrying out programmes in line with the objectives of regional planning policies can be temporarily exempted
from the business license tax ("patente") and may be granted a reduction of transfer duty.

C. FINANCIAL INSTRUMENTS

The object of the instruments considered so far was to promote
self-financing or to raise enterprises' self-financing ratio and, by
so doing, to try to exert some influence on the volume of investment
needed to raise production capacity and employment. In some cases,
this quantitative incentive has been modified through the action of
eligibility criteria, according to the type of activity considered,
the branch of industry concerned or the region intended to receive
this investment.

Self-financing can influence not only the volume of self-
financed investment, but also the volume of investment financed with
the help of outside capital inasmuch as companies rarely finance investment wholly from own resources. In many cases of investment pre-
senting a particular risk, access to outside sources of finance can
depend on the size of the contribution from own resources.

At Central Government level, the need to improve means of action
has led to financial instruments often being used in conjunction with
fiscal instruments. In the first place, despite the fact that fiscal
techniques are relatively flexible in conception, some countries did
not fail to mention fairly major difficulties encountered in applying
certain instruments of a fiscal nature and, above all, in keeping a
check of the anticipated effects, particularly in view of the complexity of all forms of company taxation. The experiment carried out
by the Canadian authorities and aimed at obtaining information on the
impact of one type of fiscal measure by means of surveys backed up
by interviews in enterprises, remains very much the exception.
Secondly, since, because of demand trends, self-financing does not
necessarily result in an optimum distribution of investment, the
public authorities make it their business to develop instruments of
a nature such as to give them the right to keep a check on the trend
of investment structures:

- by giving direct financial aid in the form of premiums and grants, etc., in other words by transferring public funds to supplement the firm's own resources;
- by making loans on normal market terms or on concessionary terms as regards rates of interest, repayment periods and instalments;
- by granting interest rebates or other forms of interest rate relief which lower the cost of credit and thus the threshold at which the investment becomes profitable;
- by giving government guarantees and thus enabling firms to borrow from financial institutions on better terms.

In some cases the total amount of aid, which varies according to the country and the instrument, may be determined by setting time limits for the measures concerned or else laying down a maximum total figure for them. It is more general for neither date nor ceiling to be set, and in these cases the assistance given is limited solely by the terms on which it is granted.

There are procedures which allow financial instruments to be used in such a way as to take account of self-financing without penalising it. In Belgium, for example, the interest relief - the difference between the rate charged by the lender and that paid by the borrower - is paid to the credit institution concerned. The State can, inter alia, give its guarantee for the repayment of principal and the payment of interest and charges in respect of the loans that are granted. For approved projects that are wholly self-financed, firms may receive a capital grant equivalent to the interest rebate so that firms relying solely on their own funds are not penalised.

Financial instruments differ from fiscal instruments in a number of ways. In the first place, as was stressed above, to the extent that a fiscal instrument has either a direct or an indirect effect on an enterprise's taxable profits, whether or not the enterprise can use these benefits depends on whether it is making a profit. Secondly, even when the application of an instrument is subject to agreement or authorisation, it would seem that fiscal instruments are aimed primarily at a group of enterprises, irrespective in many cases of the nature of their activities, even though the criteria determining their eligibility often vary according to the type of investment: buildings, plant, etc. Taxation also seems to have an essentially indirect impact on investment by virtue of its influence on an enterprise's cash flow through book entries. It would therefore appear to favour enterprises at the expense of projects, and by the same token make it very difficult for the public authorities to institute methods of surveillance. Lastly, it transpires that it is difficult to assess the benefit thus granted, and its limitations as an incentive are fairly soon realised. How is it possible to evaluate the

advantages that an enterprise may derive from having financial resources at its disposal now rather than at some future time, and can
the taxation advantages available to a group of enterprises reasonably
be extended, even temporarily, without unbalancing the structure of
budgetary revenue?

As has already been indicated, fiscal instruments often seem
to be used as a means of stabilizing the cyclical situation. This
can in itself have a number of consequences of a structural nature
because of its more or less marked effect on this or that type of
enterprise (depending, for example, on how capital intensive it is)
or industry (e.g. capital goods). Is this to imply that financial
instruments are more frequently used for structural purposes? Judging from the information submitted by the countries, this would seem
on the whole to be the case. If so, it is doubtless because of the
difficulties of implementing in a very short space of time - i.e. at
a given moment during a rapidly changing economic situation - financial instruments based on examination and decision-making procedures
for handling a large number of additional applications made by
enterprises.

An exceptional example of cyclical use is provided by the
financial assistance introduced by the <u>Swedish</u> authorities and designed to increase stockpiling during an unfavourable economic situation in order to maintain the level of stocks. Companies which could
show proof of an increase in stocks and of maintaining their work-
forces at 1st November, 1971 level received a grant of up to 20 per
cent of the value of the increase in stocks.

Judging from the information received, it would seem that financial instruments are very often used for regional development.
Since the regional aspect does not come within the compass of this
report, the following paragraphs will only consider the general side
of promoting productive investment, though it is understood that non-
specific assistance restricted to certain regions can, because of the
existing or future industrial structures of these regions, have the
same effect as specific assistance to the extent that the level of
aid is more than sufficient to offset the disincentives stemming from
conditions peculiar to the regions.

In <u>Germany</u>, the possibility of loans or interest relief exists
but only grants and guarantees have so far been used to promote productive investment. These account for nearly 80 per cent of the
cost of German regional policy which is mainly concerned with the
areas on its Eastern borders whose distance from the main centres,
coupled with the way in which the country is divided, is conducive
to economic decline. However, other areas threatened with under-
employment have also been assisted in this way. Two types of subsidy
have been in existence since 1969. One, a grant by the tax

51

authorities out of tax revenue (and therefore classed as a fiscal instrument in the country's reply), amounts to 7.5 per cent of the value of the investment. The other consists of subsidies which can range between 15 and 25 per cent of the investment cost of the projects financed by the Federal Government and the Länder in 327 developed centres. The latter measure is said to have helped finance investment worth DM.40,800 million covering about 17,000 projects, for the two years 1972 and 1975 put together. It is claimed that 419,000 new jobs were created and 404,000 safeguarded over the same period. The German authorities spent 532 million each year to achieve this result, since 1975 DM.588 million. Part of this amount can be used by local authorities for the development of industry-related infrastructure.

In Finland interest reliefs have gradually taken the place of grants as a way of assisting regional development in recent years. Under the 1969 Act on the promotion of economic activities in development areas, interest relief varying from area to area reduces the cost of loans raised from private or public banks or from foreign financial institutions. In this case the Government guarantees the loans. In the most under-developed area, relief is given for the whole of the interest during the first two years and amounts to 50 per cent during the next two years. In the next area in order of development, the corresponding figures are 80 and 40 per cent; Mks.150 million have been earmarked for such loans in 1974 and about Mks.29 million for interest relief.

On the expiry of the 1969 Act, a new act of very similar content will be proposed for the period 1975-1979. According to the Bill, Government subsidies for investment and training in development regions will replace the interest relief provided for in the 1969 Act.

In France, the State may grant aid to encourage regional development. Such aid essentially consists of premiums of three types: premiums for regional development, premiums for the siting of tertiary activities and premiums for the siting of research activities. Premiums for regional development, instituted in 1972, may be granted to enterprises which establish new activities or extend them to areas with special employment problems, for an investment of at least Fr.500,000 leading to the creation of at least thirty jobs, or in the case of conversion to the maintenance of this number. Programmes which have the effect of increasing the staff employed in a single establishment by at least 30 per cent or by at least 100 persons may also qualify. The amount of the premium depends on the location or on the nature of the investment. The ceiling for the premium is Fr.15,000 per job in the case of creation and Fr.12,000 per job in the case of extension of an activity. Premium for the siting of tertiary activities may be awarded to enterprises which propose to

create or decentralise their general services in certain areas.
Investments for which such a premium may be granted must be in a regional city or in an area receiving regional development assistance.
They must result in the establishment of at least 100 permanent jobs
and of at least 50 in the case of research and development departments
or operations involving the transfer of head offices. The rate
ranges from 10 to 20 per cent, depending on the type of investment.
Premiums for the siting of research activities may be granted to
establishments investing for the purpose of setting up or extending
research activities. The rate for this premium is 15 to 20 per cent
of the total investment. It cannot be added to other premiums for
regional development.

From 1972 to 1974 the trend of aid granted under the heading of
these three premiums was as follows:

	1972	1973	1974
Premiums for regional development:			
Number (units)	493	597	469
Amount (millions of francs)	274.9	422.7	392.0
Number of jobs created (units)	n.s.	47,771	37,823
Premiums for the siting of tertiary activities:			
Number (units)	5	6	10
Amount (millions of francs)	10.4	4.7	18.2
Number of jobs created (units)	n.s.	887	1,540
Premiums for the siting of research activities:			
Number (units)	-	-	1
Amount (millions of francs)			0.4

In France, aid for the development of the Overseas Departments
can take the form of capital subsidies or tax allowances. Under the
heading of measures designed to help achieve the targets laid down
in the Plan with regard to capital projects, capital and employment
grants can be allocated by the Fonds d'Investissement des Départements
d'Outre-Mer (FIDOM) to enterprises investing in these Départements.

Tax legislation comprises a great many measures designed to encourage economic and social development in the Overseas Departments.
Some are of automatic and general application, such, in particular,
as the reduction in the rates of VAT, income tax or the corporation
tax base.

There are in France two specific forms of aid proper, one for
the South-West region, and the other for Brittany. The "Centime
du Sud-Ouest" was introduced when the Lacq field began to be
worked. It is financed by means of a support fund supplied by
a levy on the royalties owed to the Government by the Société
nationale des Pétroles d'Aquitaine as the holder of mining concessions. The assistance is given to companies which are users of
natural gas and are located in the South West regions, in order to

lower the price of the gas they consume. The "Franc breton". The object of this aid, which dates from 1962, is to encourage new enterprises or the expansion of existing enterprises in Brittany by granting them a subsidy based on consumption of high voltage electricity, and fixed at 1 centime per kilowatt-hour of new or additional consumption.

In addition to the financial aid for regional purposes mentioned in the preceding paragraph, the French public authorities may grant loans to industrial firms out of FDES resources for carrying out investment projects intended to meet objectives under the Plan or for launching specific actions, as for purposes of decentralisation, the conversion of activities, increasing their productivity or restructuring. As loans in recent years have essentially been granted for restructuring operations, the latter will be considered in greater detail in Part II of the report.

Financial assistance may also take the form of credits for promoting industrial policy. The purpose of these credits is to facilitate the development of progressive industrial firms or of key sectors capable of influencing the entire industrial fabric and of helping the balance of foreign trade. Such aid may also be given to firms in difficult straits. The aid agreements prescribe either the terms of repayment or a government share in the profits, as the case may be. Aid granted in 1974 comes under two types of programme:

1. Specific programmes, which are programmes of a national character conducted jointly with other ministerial departments. Particular instances are the "Copper Plan", the "Measurement Action", the programme for promoting industrial automation, the promotion of numerically controlled machine tools and the Secam system;
2. General programmes, whose purpose is continuous adjustment of the machinery for industrial production to changing economic conditions in the short or medium term.

Credits granted under specific programmes amounted to some Frs.36 million in 1973 and 1974, while those under the general programmes rose from Frs.57.7 million in 1973 to 111.2 million in 1974.

In Sweden, state financial aid is directed towards grants and loans with the object of promoting investment in certain regions. The following Table summarises the use made of this aid and its effects. Between 1965 and 30th June, 1973, S.Kr.425 million were given and S.Kr.1,653 million were lent to 947 firms, enabling them to acquire equipment and durables to a value of S.Kr.3,500 million, thus contributing to the creation of 18,051 new jobs (see Table 7).

In the United Kingdom, the then Government outlined in its White Paper "Industrial Regional Development", published in March 1972,

TABLE 7

SWEDEN

REGIONAL LOANS AND GRANTS: THEIR USE AND EFFECTS

REGIONAL DEVELOPMENT AID	1970/71	1971/72	1972/73	1.7.1965 - 30/6/1973
Grants (S.Kr. million)	67	72	80	425
Loans (S.Kr. million)	336	269	261	1,653
Total (S.Kr. million)	403	341	341	2,078
Total cost of investment projects involved (S.Kr. million)				ca.3,500(1)
Number of firms assisted	225	274	363	947
Average amount per firm (S.Kr.000)	1,791	1,245	939	21,947(2)
Expected increase in employment				26,157
Actual increase in employment				18,081
Cost of aid per job created (S.Kr.000)				114.9

(1) Up to 31st December, 1972.

(2) Firms assisted in more than one way are nevertheless counted only once.

55

a number of measures aimed at stimulating industrial and regional growth. Some of the measures were implemented in the Finance Act 1972 (see fiscal instruments), and the remainder in the Industry Act of the same year. This latter Act provided for aids to regional development through productive investment falling mainly under two headings: general aid in the form of Regional Development Grants and selective assistance under the heading of Section 7 of the Industry Act 1972, which could take several forms.

Regional development grants are payable at a rate of 20 per cent towards approved capital expenditure in the development and intermediate areas and at a rate of 22 per cent in the special development areas on providing new buildings or works (excluding mining works) on premises used wholly or mainly for carrying on qualifying activities (principally manufacturing, mining and construction). In the special development and development areas grants are also payable at rates of 22 per cent and 20 per cent respectively towards approved capital expenditure on mining works and on new plant and machinery for use on premises used wholly or mainly for the qualifying activities. For the construction industry, the grant may be paid on approved capital expenditure on new plant and machinery provided for use in the special development areas and the development areas even though its use may not be confined to specified qualifying premises in those areas. If it is not so confined, however, the rate of grant is 20 per cent whether or not the plant and machinery is used in the special development areas. The system, which is administered by the Department of Industry came into force on 22nd March, 1972. In November 1975 time limits for the receipt of applications for specified periods relating to provisions of assets were announced and came into operation for the first period on 1st July, 1976 (on assets provided up to 31st March, 1974). Part I of the Industry Act contains no clause stipulating Government holdings in the equity of subsidised industrial enterprises nor is there any requirement to provide additional employment. In general, grants are made on condition that the assets in question are used for which the grant was given during a minimum of four years and they are repayable in whole or in part if the assets are not so used. Although the total of grants paid in the first financial year 1972/73 amounted to the relatively small total of £8.1 million this went up in 1974/75 to £212.8 million and is expected to increase to a range between £350 and £400 million each year. Assuming the standard rate of 20 per cent, total assisted capital expenditure should amount to approximately £1.7 - £2 billion per year.

As far as Regional Selective Assistance is concerned, two main types of project qualify: projects which create new jobs (category A) and modernisation and rationalisation measures which maintain employment levels (category B). Category A projects qualify for:

- loans at concessionary rates of interest (at present 10 per
  cent) with the possibility of an initial moratorium on interest payments, not normally exceeding two years;
- interest relief grants, as an alternative to loans. The present basic rate of the grant is three per cent per year of the
  reference loan for up to four years. However, if the enterprise has had the benefit of a grace period free of interest,
  the grant can go up to 12 per cent for two years and then
  three per cent for four years;
- removal grants for enterprises which leave non-assisted areas
  in order to set up in assisted areas. These grants can amount
  to 80 per cent of the cost of transferring plant, machinery,
  stock and raw material from the old location to the new one,
  and of the regulation compensation for dismissal paid by the
  employer to staff who do not wish to follow the enterprise.

Category B projects can receive assistance in the form of government
loans on virtually commercial terms (at present 13.5 per cent), when
funds have not been found on the capital market. The figures in
Table 8 show how Regional Selective Assistance has operated between
its introduction in 1972 and 31st March, 1976.

Following the publication of the White Paper on 'Investment
Incentives' in October 1970 which announced the then Government's
intention to replace investment grants payable under the Industrial
Development Act 1966 by a system of tax allowances and reductions in
order to help create the conditions for increasing investment, these
grants were abolished by the Investment and Building Grants Act 1971
in respect of expenditure incurred on or after 27 October 1970 unless
it consists of a sum or sums payable under a contract made on or before 26 October 1970. The Act also made provision for the imposition
of terminal dates by which applications have to be received in respect
of specified periods of expenditure. Grants are paid at a rate of
20 per cent (40 per cent in the development areas) in respect of
capital expenditure incurred in providing new plant and machinery to
firms engaged in qualifying processes of manufacture, extraction and
construction and for the provision of ships, hovercraft and computers
and on mining works. In each of the financial years 1969/70 and
1970/71 the total grant paid was approximately £587 million but following the regulations introduced in 1970 the total amount fell to
£336 million in 1972/73 and to £119 million in 1974/75. The regional
share of grants paid in respect of plant, machinery, computers and
mining works is usually between 40 to 50 per cent of the total.

Whether physical or financial, the instruments considered so
far, which were designed to increase production capacity and create
or preserve jobs, mainly affected investment, considering that investment was bound in time to create jobs. It has already been seen

57

Table 8

UNITED KINGDOM

INDUSTRY ACT 1972

REGIONAL SELECTIVE ASSISTANCE

(Section 7)

1972 – 31st March, 1976

I. Applications accepted

    (a) Loans made, etc.

Number of loans	485
Total amount involved (£ million)	97.4
Number of interest relief grants	1,758
Total amount involved (£ million)	86.4
Number of removal grants	315
Total amount involved (£ million)	5.9

    (b) Effects:

Total project costs (£ million)	1911.4
Number of jobs associated with the applications	186,000
Number of jobs maintained	68,000

II. Applications in hand at 31st March, 1976

Number of applications in hand	359
Number of jobs associated with these applications	23,000

that a distinction had to be made in this respect between various types of investment, the job content of which could vary considerably and even be negative.

In the United Kingdom, the regional employment premium which dates back to 1967, is designed to reduce employment disparities between the development areas and the rest of the country by directly influencing the employment factor. It is paid to employers in these areas in the form of a weekly sum of £3 for each adult male worker, £1.50 for youths and women, 95 pence for girls and half this sum for part-time employees. A study made by the Department of Applied Economics at Cambridge University estimates the number of new jobs created in this way up until 1970 at 20,000 to 50,000. The following table shows the amounts paid in the development areas and the average number of employees.

The "investment" factor can also contain an element of technological progress in that new plant usually incorporates new technological developments or allows production of new products or products improved in various ways: quality, safety, savings in energy or raw materials, for example. The public authorities have therefore turned their attention more specifically to promoting the technological factor in general.

UNITED KINGDOM

REGIONAL EMPLOYMENT PREMIUM

Year	Amount (£ million)	Average number of jobs
1967/68	34	−
1968/69	102	−
1969/70	108	1,573,442
1970/71	108	1,591,207
1971/72	108	1,596,778
1972/73	100	1,488,116
1973/74	106	1,500,974

Chapter 4

INTRODUCTION OF NEW PRODUCTS OR PROCESSES

A. NATURE OF THE PROBLEM

While it should be possible to finance investment for production
purposes from a combination of self-financing and the capital market,
in the broadest sense, inasmuch as this investment does not normally
involve an excessive risk for the investor since the goods produced
are marketed within a short space of time, investment for research
and development involves risks of a different kind which can demand
specific assistance from the public authorities. The difference can
lie first of all in the length of time between the conception of the
idea and the development of an industrial prototype, and again between the prototype and its acceptance by the market which depends,
in particular, on its cost. Secondly, the difference can be in the
uncertainty which grows admittedly with the passage of time, but
also because of ignorance as to whether it will be accepted by the
market. Over and above these risk factors, it can be said that the
public authorities have tended increasingly to intervene. On the
one hand they have established specific objectives for industrial
policy such as increased competitiveness, improved efficiency,
greater potential for national industrial technology and the promotion of production capacities employing highly skilled labour.
These objectives have recently been supplemented by those relating
to savings in energy and raw materials. On the other hand, with
general well-being in mind, the public authorities have defined targets in areas such as work or product safety and the protection of
the environment, and in so doing they have introduced constraints
compelling enterprises to use new products or processes which will
enable them to achieve these targets. These targets or processes
can exist at the prototype stage, for example, and in this case the
problem is the cost of introduction, or they may not yet exist - at
least not in this advanced form - in which case the innovation process should be started from the beginning, often with pre-established
time limits.

Thus, the introduction of new products and processes represents
a cost which is traditionally financed from self-financing, i.e.
mainly by the client and the shareholder, since the nature of the
risk greatly restricts the possibility of achieving objectives by
means of outside capital - from the bank system for example. However, since the objectives are fixed by governments, the latter have
given themselves the means by which to achieve them and, by the same
token, influence the financing of the innovation process by themselves financing all or part of the risks incurred by enterprises.

This action can take various forms. In the first place, governments can assume responsibility for all financing by having their
own installations carry out the studies and research needed in order
to ensure that enterprises subsequently benefit from the findings.
This type of procedure relates more especially to so-called funda-
mental research. Secondly, the public authorities can help to
finance R & D in industrial enterprises, either in a general way by
encouraging the creation of or annual increases in R & D budgets, or
more specifically at different stages and in different ways, the two
often being very much interdependent. An initial stage is that of
the purchase by the enterprise of the buildings and plant necessary
in order to create or develop a research centre. The public authorities can recognise the specific nature of plant and equipment from
the point of view of its profitability by authorising exceptional
depreciation rates. The limits of fiscal mechanisms have already
been discussed in a general way above. A second stage consists of
one or more enterprises defining a research project which they then
apply to have co-financed by the public authorities. For this type
of assistance, the latter have established financial instruments
which, taking into account the nature of the risk incurred and the
progress of the research, usually take the form of a subsidy or of
aid which is repayable in the event of the results being marketed
successfully, i.e. a contractual relationship can be established between the Government and the enterprise. By less direct means involving the modification of legal and fiscal structures, the
Government can encourage research co-operation between firms or make
it easier to have it financed by an entire industry. Some types of
instruments make special or exclusive allowance for that intangible
factor which is the contribution that research workers make to a
project by participating in expenditure on staff employed on approved
projects. The third stage is to disseminate the findings, either by
encouraging information or, more directly, by providing financial
assistance for enterprises capable of using the new product or
process.

Government action in the research and development field has
changed over the course of time. Initially restricted to certain

preferential industries, R & D assistance is tending to become more and more general. The following paragraphs deal separately with aid for industry as a whole and assistance given to specific branches of industry. As regards the latter more especially, all firms, regardless of size and of the industry they are in, qualify for such assistance provided their projects are accepted

B. FISCAL INSTRUMENTS

Fiscal instruments, and in particular accelerated depreciation, may be an effective stimulus for acquiring the assets necessary for R & D. In the United Kingdom, for example, the 1968 Capital Allowances Act provides that expenditure on the provision of scientific research equipment can be fully written off in the first year.

In Australia too, all branches of industry can qualify for R & D assistance in the form of special fiscal depreciation. This depreciation applies only to factories and machinery used solely for R & D purposes, and is fixed at 50 per cent using the decreasing balance method of depreciation or 33 1/3 per cent using linear depreciation. An additional tax allowance in the form of three equal annual deductions can be used for capital expenditure on buildings used exclusively for scientific research related to the activity of the taxpayer.

In Spain a decree of July 1975 provides for a specific tax treatment of technology and other services relating to goods in foreign trade. A measure of December 1974 on the special registration of the electronics and telecommunications industries supplements the decision taken in July 1974 which had declared to be of preferential interest the manufacture of electronic apparatus and equipment and their components.

In Japan, various fiscal techniques are used to encourage R & D activities. They largely consist of credit against tax, a special deduction from taxable profits, and possibilities of additional depreciation. For example, if R & D expenditure in one financial year exceeds the maximum figure under this heading in any previous year, a credit is given against corporation tax of an amount equal to 25 per cent of the difference or 10 per cent of the tax, whichever is less. This measure, introduced in 1967, is to apply up to and including 1975. A special deduction from taxable profits may also be attracted by part of the proceeds of the sale of patent rights or the licensing of industrial property rights abroad. This deduction may amount to as much as 50 per cent of the total ordinary income. This measure was introduced in 1969 and should normally come to an end in fiscal year 1975. Likewise, from 1958 on, firms have been

able to take advantage of an additional first-year writing-down allowance over and above normal depreciation, equivalent to one-third
of the cost of machinery that has received a government "new technology" certificate.

In Sweden, there is a fiscal technique which is particularly
designed for the manpower, i.e. "grey matter", component of expenditure on research and development and, after authorisation, R & D
expenditure abroad. The measure was introduced in 1973 and applies,
under certain conditions, to all taxpayers engaged in industrial
production who will have R & D costs during the period 1973-1980.
The deduction is double: the first is equal to ten per cent of five-
thirds of wage costs of all kinds net of the costs or the purchase
of the proceeds of the sale of patent rights and increased after
authorisation, by R & D costs incurred abroad. The second, which is
equal to 20 per cent, can after authorisation be added to this; it
is calculated on the basis of the difference over two years between
the sums brought out in the accounts for calculating the first deduction. This instrument also acts, therefore, as an incentive to
increase R & D costs.

C. FINANCIAL INSTRUMENTS

However, these fiscal techniques have only limited application,
principally because they can only benefit firms that make profits.
For this reason, some countries have given them up in favour of
financial aid which is more flexible in its use and more specific
in its orientation. It should however be emphasized that this soon
comes up against two limitations, particularly with regard to orientation. Government financial assistance applies, with certain exceptions (see the case of Canada with the IRDIA and Australia with
the SRDG), to specific projects which are normally submitted to it
by enterprises, and as a supplement in that the financing share
cannot normally exceed a certain percentage of the total cost.
Government action therefore has to remain within strict bounds. Research which exceeds enterprises' financing capacity, either individually or in combination, and whose prospects of becoming profitable
within given time limits are very hypothetical military or civil
research: space, aeronautics for example are not subject to these
limits . This trend is particularly well illustrated by the examples
of Germany and Canada.

In Germany, the right to write-down up to 50 per cent of the
cost of moveable assets acquired for R & D activities over the first
five years was abolished at the end of 1974. The same applies to
buildings where the rate was 30 per cent. In view of the administrative difficulties of the system, the Federal Government considers it

preferable to assist research through investment grants and to disregard the fiscal situation of the firm submitting a project. These grants may cover up to 7.5 per cent of the cost of acquisition or construction. The scheme has been in operation since 1970, and from 1975 onwards wholly replaced the accelerated depreciation mechanism. The Federal Government considers the grant to be fiscal in nature. Administered by the tax authorities, it is paid out of the revenue from tax on industrial profits. The tax revenue lost was DM.140 million in 1971, DM.155 million in 1972, DM.215 million in 1973, DM.240 million in 1974 and DM.85 million in 1975.

In Canada, the Industrial Research & Development Incentives Act (IRDIA) was introduced in 1967 to replace the stipulations regarding incentives for scientific R & D contained in the 1962-1966 Income Tax Act. This was in recognition of the need to reduce the disadvantages of the fiscal measures which had the effect of depriving enterprises not subject to the tax of the benefit of the measures. The object of the IRDIA programme is to encourage Canadian enterprises to pursue their research and development activities along lines which should bring Canada economic advantages via the production and sale of new or improved products or processes. This assistance is in the form of subsidies, the amount of which is determined on the basis of the level of and increase in enterprises' R & D expenditure. Since the IRDIA was introduced, more than 5,000 applications have been approved, 3,000 of them during the years 1971 to 1973/74. The approved applications have together given rise to subsidies totalling $168 million, and an increase in R & D amounting to $672 million. Because of the incentives it contains to increase R & D expenditure, the programme has been of particular interest to enterprises beginning to establish budgets for this type of activity, and to small enterprises.

In Australia, too, the approach has been one of general encouragement to increase R & D expenditure. The specific purpose of the Australian Industrial Research and Development Grants Board, which was set up in 1967, is to encourage Australian manufacturing and mining companies to increase their expenditure on research and development. The subsidies are based on a percentage of the approved expenditure incurred by the companies. In general terms, approved expenditure refers to the increase in current expenditure on R & D above the level reached in the course of a moving base year, plus capital expenditure in certain fields. The general subsidy is based on a percentage of 50 per cent of the approved expenditure up to 50,000 Australian dollars, while the selective subsidies are based on a percentage decided by the Council responsible for running the programme (according to a criterion of national interest laid down in the legislation) for expenditure exceeding Aus.$50,000. Payments, up until the end of June 1974, exceeded Aus.$73 million. In August 1973, the Government announced that there would be a review of the working and effectiveness of this programme.

Other examples of the use made of financial instruments are given below.

In Belgium, the Act of 17th July, 1959 on aid for economic growth and the creation of new industries, and that of 30th December, 1970 on economic growth, enable the public authorities to grant all applicants repayable loans (which can amount to as much as 80 per cent of expenditure) if they are intended to promote research or help perfect prototypes, new products or new manufacturing processes. This loan becomes repayable as soon as the industrial or commercial establishment reaches break-even point, or where patent rights are sold or licences granted.

In order to further research and development with regard to new products or processes, the public authorities in France grant various types of aid to industrial enterprises. The main forms consist of aid from the Research Fund, predevelopment assistance and development assistance. Aid from the Research Fund takes the form of grants for projects selected by the science committees of the Délégation Générale à la Recherche Scientifique et Technique (DGRST), in the light of the project's value, its compatibility with the research guidelines defined by this body and the quality of research teams. The maximum amount is 50 per cent of allowable expenditure. Predevelopment assistance, initiated in 1969 and expanded in 1974, is intended to promote the effective use by industry of the findings and capacities of joint research centres, and to help enterprises wishing to avail themselves of the facilities of these centres for developing an invention. Aid is in the form of a subsidy. The purpose of development assistance, created in 1965, is to help perfect new national processes and techniques for industry which appear promising from an economic standpoint. This aid covers 50 per cent of the cost of allowable expenditure under the development programme. It takes the form of a loan which is repayable in case of success. Repayment is effected by levying a percentage on turnover and on licences granted for the product or process. In case of success, repayment normally takes place within four to six years after marketing begins. Enterprises must, moreover, pay an annual royalty.

Aid granted under these three headings has been as follows:

65

PROGRAMME AUTHORISATIONS

(Millions of francs)

	1972	1973	1974
Research Fund	-	-	210.8(1)
Predevelopment assistance	8.8	10.5	13.6
Development assistance	196.7	159.7	243.2
Reimbursements	6.1	19.8	20.4

1) Public and private enterprises

The distribution by sector of aid granted from the Research Fund and of development assistance was as follows in 1974:

1974 PROGRAMME AUTHORISATION

(Millions of francs)

	Research Fund	Development
Electronics	26.1	
Metal-working	6.9	46.3
Mechanical engineering	8.7	36.3
Electrical engineering		49.3
Information		17.8
Chemicals	12.0	23.1
Food industries	4.7	
Sciences	2.7	
Energy	1.2	
Miscellaneous		21.2
Total:	62.2	194.0

In order to promote industrial research and development and to increase the pace of technological development in industry, the public authorities in Greece have introduced a measure allowing industrial and craft enterprises to deduct from their net profits, within a limit of ten per cent of the total, the value of new scientific instruments acquired between 1st January, 1973 and 31st December, 1977.

In Italy, Act No. 1089 of 25th October, 1968 concerning measures to encourage applied research and industrial development makes provision for three main types of financial intervention: 10 year loans at three per cent, the taking of holdings, and loans which are repayable in the event of success. Government assistance can amount to as much as 70 per cent of total planned expenditure. The projects submitted are examined by the Istituto di Credito Mobiliare whose conclusions are submitted to the CIPE for approval. The annual credits allocated by the Government are in the region of L.250 billion.

In Japan, in addition to the grant system introduced in 1950 (see below), one of the activities of the Development Bank is to make loans at reduced interest rates (7.5 per cent, 8.5 per cent or the general rate) to help launch advanced technologies. It also makes loans for the conversion of manufacturing processes in order to reduce pollution, for example the caustic soda industry (interest rate 7.7 per cent). In 1974, out of total loans of ¥9.8 million, approximately, 5.7 million were intended to promote advanced technology.

The system of grants introduced in 1950, and since enlarged, is designed to help introduce production processes based on more efficient and less polluting technologies. The rate of the grant varies between 50 and 75 per cent of expenditure depending on its purpose, for example the development of closed circuit production processes. For 1974, a sum of ¥4,240 million was earmarked in the budget under this heading.

In Norway, the Institute for the Public Financing of Industrial R & D was set up in 1965 with capital of some N.Kr.130 million made up from budgetary funds over several years. The Institute grants medium-term credits for financing industrial R & D projects up to a maximum of 50 per cent of the estimated expenditure. If the project or projects assisted in this way should prove commercial failures, the Institute may abandon all or part of the debts owed to it. It therefore participates in the risks of an operation, while the borrower can exploit the results as he likes.

In Sweden, the Board for Technical Development (STU) set up in 1968, is the central authority responsible for administering public authority aid for technical research and industrial development. The forms that this aid can take are fairly flexible: loans and loans which are repayable in the event of the investment proving profitable, for example. The STU administers several programmes which amounted to an estimated S.Kr.205 million in 1974/75.

In order partially to overcome these limitations, the public authorities in some countries have resorted to the principle of the plan or concerted action. This approach allows the Government to intervene early in the conception of a research programme or even to take the initiative in this respect. This seems to be the case in Spain and France.

In Spain, where industrialisation is fairly recent and perhaps more rapid for this reason, and where the public authorities have often used the "plan" concept, or a planned concerted approach, the various components of a plan and, consequently, of the instruments it employs cannot always be distinguished with sufficient clarity. On the one hand, substantial sections of industry must resort to various types of aid, including industrial R & D, in order to become

modern and competitive at international level. On the other hand,
the very notion of a "plan" implies the use of many different instruments including those relating to technology. The Spanish authorities therefore consider that concerted sectoral measures and
the National Industrial Institute also contribute, each in their own
way, to the technological development of Spanish industry. These
two instruments will be considered below under the heading of structural adaptation. Various legislative provisions concerning the
"mixed manufacturing system" may be mentioned here. This system
was introduced by Decree Law of 30th June, 1967. It is applicable
to industrialisation or the improvement of manufacturing or service
installations. Under this system national producers work together
with foreign producers in the production of capital goods, the latter
supplying the former with new techniques or parts which are not made
in Spain and which are of special value owing to the effects they
can have on the productivity of machines resulting from such co-
operation. It is for this reason that any equipment or machine,
whether made to order or mass produced, may be of mixed manufacture.
The principles which govern mixed manufacturing or the conditions
which must be fulfilled if it is to take place may be summarised as
follows:

  a) the manufacture of some of the components of the equipment
     must not yet have been started in Spain;
  b) there must exist a strong economic advantage for undertaking
     their manufacture in Spain.

The main applications of mixed manufacturing are as set out
below:

Thermal Power Stations	Miscellaneous
Ventilators	Asphalting installations
Coal crushers	Marine steam turbines
Condensers	Motor-driven pumps for marine purposes
Travelling grates	
Refineries and Petrochemical Plants	Propane storage tanks
Trays and racks for cracking towers	Hydraulic turbines
Boilers for synthetic resins	Rectifiers for galvanising plant
Iron and Steel Industry	
Furnaces for the iron and steel industry	

In France, the public authorities have introduced a distinction
between research and development instruments and those relating to
innovation. As far as research is concerned, aid granted to competitive industries is dispensed according to the following procedures

1. Concerted action by the DGRST: on the recommendation of a
   scientific committee, these measures finance part of the expenditure by one or more laboratories for the purpose of
   research work carried out under the heading of a programme
   recognised to be of priority importance. Government assistance can range, depending upon where the research is carried out, between 50 per cent of the total cost of the
   project for industrial enterprises, 75 per cent (in general)
   of the total cost in the case of industrial technical
   centres and research firms under contract, and 100 per cent
   of the direct cost of research in the case of government
   laboratories.
2. Pre-development aid is used to finance experiments with new
   products or processes established in an Industrial Technical
   Centre.
3. Assistance at the development stage can be used to subsidise
   up to 50 per cent of the total cost of developing an innovation (research, realisation, prototype testing), in return
   for a fee and repayment in the event of success by means of
   a levy on the turnover which is effected at the time of
   marketing.

Differential impact

   Available in theory to all enterprises, the way in which an
instrument is conceived can influence its impact. This differential
impact can be explicit but seems in most cases to be implicit. It
is important to have knowledge of it when assessing how an instrument
is functioning in relation to its objective. The impact can vary
according to the size of the recipient enterprise, which is partly
the case in Germany and also in Canada for the IRAP and, conversely,
for other programmes: PAIT and IDAP; or according to the industry -
again the example of Canada (IRAP) and Finland, for example, comes
to mind; or again according to whether or not industrial R & D budgets are growing - the example of Australia has already been
mentioned. In this last case, it would seem that the impact has been
twofold: on the one hand the system tends to encourage enterprises
to introduce R & D budgets since their inexistence is more charac-
teristic of certain sizes of enterprise and certain industries, and
on the other hand it tends to favour enterprises with rapidly expanding budgets.

   Thus, in Germany, 80 per cent of the firms that have been receiving R & D promotion grants have staffs of under 500. Grants
under this scheme, introduced in 1972, cover up to 50 per cent of
the cost of projects approved by the Ministry of Economic Affairs.
In 1972-1975, 186 firms applied. Out of the 105 cases considered,

81 were approved. About DM.38 million was paid out to finance projects totalling about DM.85 million.

In Canada, the oldest existing programme - the Industrial Research Assistance Programme (IRAP) - which was set up in 1962 and is administered by the National Research Council of Canada, provides for the granting of subsidies to authorised research workers engaged in approved research projects and, by so doing, explicitly recognises the weight and role of research workers in R & D budgets. The subsidy covers the wage costs of hired staff and the participation of professors and consultants. From the introduction of the programme in 1962 up until 31st March, 1974, approved expenditure totalled Can.$67.2 million for 566 projects amounting to a total cost of Can.$165.8 million, i.e. about 40 per cent of government aid. From 1969/70 until 1973/74, between 22 per cent and 32 per cent of this aid went to the chemical and pharmaceutical industries, between 13 and 23 per cent to the electrical and electronics industries and between 9 and 13 per cent to the pulp and paper industry. During the same period, the share received by enterprises employing fewer than 200 people rose from 27 to 45 per cent of the total.

Still in Canada, and to some extent unlike the IRAP, financial aid under the Programme for the Advancement of Industrial Technology (PAIT) and the Industrial Design Assistance Programme (IDAP) seems to have gone mainly to bigger firms. The PAIT was introduced in 1965 and has been available to industrial and mining firms since 1970 in the form of subsidies which can amount to up to 50 per cent of the cost of the approved project. From 1965 to 1970, this aid was in the form of loans. Between 1971/72 and 1973/74, 424 projects received assistance worth a total of some $132 million. Up until the end of 1972/73, the main industry to benefit was the electrical and electronics industry, and more than 50 per cent of the funds went to enterprises with an annual turnover of more than Can.$5 million. The IDAP, which was introduced in 1970, obviously has more limited objectives which are to improve the design of Canadian products and therefore reduce their cost. Contributions can amount to a maximum of 50 per cent of the operational and administrative cost of the project. The main recipient industries have been wood products, engineering, machinery and plant and transport, while in the case of firms, the bulk has gone to those with an annual turnover of more than Can.$1 million.

In Finland, contracts placed by the Ministry for Trade and Industry are also designed to encourage R & D activities conducive to the rational use of energy, better use of indigenous raw materials and energy resources in order to reduce imports. The Government finances up to half the cost of research. Between 1969 and 1973, 639 contracts were concluded worth F.Mk.59.8 million. Budget credits

amounted to F.Mk.24.5 million. Since 1969, the main recipient industries have been the metal processing industries (38 per cent) and the
electrical engineering industry (23 per cent), followed by the wood
products and chemical industries.

The Finnish National Research and Development Fund, set up in
1967, makes loans and grants to help finance projects whose value to
society is clearly demonstrable.

Most countries have been obliged to promote certain sectors in
order to achieve what are considered to be priority objectives in
the national interest. Some of these objectives are not directly
economic, e.g. defence and aerospace research. Others have more immediate economic relevance, and certain governments have therefore
given their backing to high-cost, high-risk investment projects in
new technologies whose purpose is to maintain the international competitiveness of advanced technology sectors such as the aerospace and
data processing industries.

Introduced in 1959, the purpose of the Canadian DIP (Defense
Industry Productivity Programme) is to increase the technological
potential of industries involved in national defence. Firms whose
projects are approved receive financial aid. Between 1959 and
31st March, 1973, grants and loans totalled $302 million. During
the last three years, amounts expended totalled $48.8 million for
1971-1972, $48.3 million for 1972-73 and $57.7 million for 1973-74.
The aerospace industry and naval dockyards (61 per cent) and electrical engineering and electronics (31 per cent) between them accounted for nearly all the finance involved (92 per cent).

Apart from their close links with the needs of national defence,
certain industries appear to hold the key to future economic development. Assistance is given to the aerospace and computer industries
in four of the countries replying to the Industry Committee's questionnaire: Canada, France, Germany and the United Kingdom.

In Germany, within the scope of the second Data Processing
Support Programme (1971-1975), grants and credits repayable in certain cases only were given for:

- market-related technical development between 1971 and 1973 at
  the amount of DM.108.7 million, in 1974 at the amount of
  DM.36.9 million and in 1975 at the amount of DM.47.8 million;
- industrial research and future-oriented development in the
  field of electronic data processing between 1971 and 1973 at
  the amount of DM.393.5 million, in 1974 at the amount of
  DM.116.0 million and in 1975 at the amount of DM.129.2 million;
- the development of modern applications of electronic data
  processing between 1971 and 1973 at the amount of DM.195 million, in 1974 at the amount of DM.103.8 million and in 1975
  at the amount of DM.150.2 million.

71

The Third Data Processing Support Programme (1976-1979) provides for
the promotion of industrial research and development in 1976 an amount
of DM.140.3 million, in 1977 an amount of DM.133.0 million, in 1978
an amount of DM.138.0 million and in 1979 an amount of DM.143.0 million. As from mid-1975, only a 50 per cent grant will normally be
made. In the case of market-related projects the recipients of a
grant are obliged to repay the relevant amount. By its third Data
Processing Support Programme the Federal Government intends to contribute to the establishment of a computer industry by the beginning
of the 1980s which:

- secures a sufficient amount of competition in all product
  areas - except superscale computers;
- is able to develop, to produce and to offer the computer system and equipment required by the public sector and by trade
  and industry;
- is viable by itself and thus independent of governmental funding
- offers highly qualified employment;
- disposes of the necessary knowledge and capabilities for the
  interaction of data processing, communications technology and
  other technologies of information processing.

Within the scope of the Third Data Processing Support Programme
further funds are planned for the promotion of the application of
data processing, i.e. in 1976 at the amount of DM.127.6 million, in
1977 at the amount of DM.133.0 million, in 1978 at the amount of
DM.144.0 million and in 1979 at the amount of DM.157.0 million. The
promotion of the application of data processing is to assist directly
work flows at the individual work place in order to make use of new
possibilities of data processing which is decentrally organised and
related to the relevant task. Moreover, this measure provides for
more direct and improved communication between the workers at their
work places and the computer systems assisting them. In addition,
it is designed to facilitate and rationalise the design of software
and its handling.

In 1968, the United Kingdom Government was instrumental in
forming "International Computer Holding" by the merger of three companies, and took holdings of 10 per cent in the new company. The new
firm received government grants totalling £13.5 million over the
period 1968-71. In addition, under the Science and Technology Act
1965, the Department of Industry is to make available to International
Computers Ltd. £40 million between 1972 and 1976 to assist the company in the development of its new range of computers. This assistance will be repayable out of profits once the new range has entered
production.

In France, the C.I.I. (Compagnie Internationale pour l'Informatique) was set up in 1967. The Government has undertaken to place research contracts worth Frs.100 million with this company each year for five years.

For the aerospace industry, however, the situation differs from country to country.

France and the United Kingdom have a big aerospace industry with a large, skilled workforce. R & D investment is increasing steeply, whilst the time-lag between aircraft design and sales is lengthening. Publicly or privately-owned firms can no longer finance all investment projects from their own resources. State aid, and sometimes international co-operation, becomes essential. The Concorde Programme is a case in point.

In Germany, government assistance to civil aviation is aimed at freeing the German aerospace industry from its complete dependence on defence orders. By encouraging firms to look for new markets which, with the development of air transport, are growing day by day, it is hoped to smooth out high-low swings in employment. Lastly, resolved to create a competitive industry capable of playing its part in international co-operation, the Federal Government pays between 60 per cent and a maximum of 90 per cent of the costs of development research. DM.190 million were paid out in 1971, DM.210 million in 1972, DM.214 million in 1973, DM.240 million in 1974 and DM.279 million in 1975. German involvement in the Airbus programme is an illustration of this policy in action.

Part II

PROMOTION OF STRUCTURAL ADAPTATION

INTRODUCTION

Structural adaptation is a vast and somewhat elusive concept. In the first place, it may be considered, from a macro-industrial point of view, as involving the reallocation of productive resources among different sectors of industrial activity. Secondly, looked at from within a given sector, it may consist of a structural mutation through merger or acquisition, or of a rationalisation of certain activities (e.g. R & D, purchasing, production, marketing) by means of co-operation or association. Finally, within the firm, structural adaptation may involve the modernisation of plant or equipment (the general concept of modernisation subsuming here the more narrowly defined activity of process innovation); and it may also mean innovation shifts, diversification or specialisation in the product line or mix. Moreover, the adaptation process may involve two or more of these aspects simultaneously.

In the two chapters which follow, it is sought, on the basis of the country replies, to link the main objectives of structural adaptation policy with the types of instruments used to attain them for the period of time covered by the replies. As already noted at the beginning of the present report, the same instrument or set of instruments may be used to attain different objectives (and, conversely), a plurality of instruments may be directed to the same objective). A clear illustration of this is provided by some national legislations, where a single legislative act may make available given incentives or aids for promoting any one or a combination of stipulated actions, such as the establishment, expansion, modernisation or conversion of production facilities. Behind this phenomenon is the fact that the specific objectives - modernisation, conversion, etc. - aimed at by specific incentives or incentive programmes are generally of an intermediate character; i.e., the attainment of these various aims is seen as contributing to more global and general (but for present purposes insufficiently specific) objectives such as, e.g., the improved international competitivity of a nation's industry.

In view of the above - and of the fact that countries may apply different conceptual designations to similar objectives, and that the various designations may be broader or narrower in scope - it was not possible for the questionnaire to establish a watertight compartmentation between the different objectives. For example, "concentration" and "cooperation" are usually forms of "rationalisation"; "modernisation" is expected to lead to "productivity improvement"; etc. The fact that countries have been free to check more than one objective for a given instrument (and to explain the purpose and scope of their instruments more fully in the descriptive part of the reply) does, of course, mitigate the inevitable constraints on the rigour possible in a study of this kind. But there do remain significant limits on the detail and analytic complexity of the picture one can draw. The two following chapters are thus structured so as to bring the country experiences within a broad framework indicating the main weight and thrust of policy instruments used to attain the principal objectives of structural adaptation as directed, respectively, to firms and to manpower.

Chapter 5

STRUCTURAL ADAPTATION OF ENTERPRISES

A. MEASURES ADDRESSED TO FIRMS IN GENERAL

A certain degree of flexibility has been introduced into the organisation of this section in order to present a profile that reflects as faithfully as possible the policy reality emerging from the country replies and that gives due attention to salient features. Thus, the first two subsections below deal with the main uses of fiscal and financial instruments to promote structural adaptation. A third subsection provides a separate discussion - merited because of the special institutional arrangements involved - of special public or semi-public bodies providing assistance of a financial character, including equity participation. Finally, a fourth subsection is concerned with the use of fiscal and financial instruments addressed to an objective which, though it is clearly relevant to the evolution of industrial structures, is not in itself of a directly structural nature: export promotion.

With specific reference to fiscal and financial instruments, both types are used to promote structural adaptation (and sometimes in conjunction with each other). However, as is clear from the discussions in the first part of this report, financial instruments seem - generally speaking - better adapted than fiscal measures to the stimulation of adaptive behaviour in a way that permits flexibility and precision in determining (within the framework set by the relevant legislation or programme) the desired points of impact (e.g., which firm, or which sectors) and the degree and structure of the aid to be provided in specific cases. Thus, the replies indicate that financial instruments are used to promote a wider range of specific forms of adaptive action. It may be added that the use of financial instruments to a significant degree, and particularly the more selective use of such instruments, would seem to be a rough indication of an "active" industrial policy or of a movement in that direction.

78

1. Fiscal instruments

Fiscal instruments, by their nature, seek to remove disincentives or possible disincentives to desired behaviour by providing for exemption from or alleviation of certain tax burdens. Analysis of the replies suggests the predominance of two types of fiscal measures to promote structural adaptation: tax abatements to encourage (i) concentration through merger or association; and (ii) the use of capital gains to promote the mobility of productive resources (apart from policies aimed at encouraging mergers). In most cases, the tax concessions apply generally to all firms, although in some instances the possibility exists of exceptional treatment on a case-by-case basis.

Concentration incentives

The specific modalities adopted to promote concentration by fiscal means vary widely from one country to another in accordance with the differences in industrial structures and in tax structures and traditions. The following illustrate the wide range of means used to attain this objective:

In France, the Act of 12th July, 1965, provides for special taxation treatment designed to encourage mergers and, when approved, the subdivision of companies and part-transfers of assets. The main provisions are as follows:

- no immediate taxation of capital gains on the various fixed assets;
- taxation in the hands of the acquiring company of net capital gains on non-depreciable fixed assets is deferred until such time as they are disposed of by the said company, such capital gains then being calculated by reference to the value of such assets as shown in the balance sheet of the company taken over;
- the requirement that capital gains (whether short or long-term) arising on depreciable assets to the merger must be added back to the acquiring company's profits taxable at the full rate of 50 per cent, is mitigated by allowing such adding back to be spread over ten years; however, the company taken over may opt for all or part of any long-term gains on its depreciable assets to be taxed in its own name at the reduced rate of 10 per cent, and in this case the capital gain on which the acquiring company has to pay a tax over ten years at 50 per cent is of course reduced to that extent;
- the acquiring company is allowed to show the depreciable assets of the company taken over at the value assigned to them for the purposes of the merger and thus to depreciate them to a

79

greater extent than would be authorised on the basis of the
value at which they were shown in the last balance sheet
drawn up for tax purposes.

Under another provision of the same Act a previous deficit incurred by a company participating in a merger may, subject to official approval, be carried forward and set off against future profits
of the acquiring company.

In Denmark, under an Act passed in 1967 the Ministry of Finance
can authorise tax exemptions on mergers between limited companies.

In Belgium, because it might otherwise retard concentration
and rationalisation, the special company income tax contribution that
is levied on any surplus arising on the division of a company's
assets ceases to be payable in certain conditions in the case of a
merger or subdivision of a company. In addition the 2 per cent
registration duty on contributions of assets in return for shares is
halved in the case of mergers where the companies concerned have
their effective registered offices in Community countries. Also,
contributions of assets for "mixed consideration" i.e. for consideration consisting in part of shares and in part of cash, debentures
or the assumption of liabilities, are not liable, in the case of a
merger, to tax on the transfer of property for valuable consideration.

In Greece, exemption may be granted, in certain conditions,
from income tax, stamp duty and transfer tax for mergers taking place
before the end of 1975. In this way it is hoped to promote the formation of companies better able to compete at international level.

In Japan, mergers between firms in the electronics and industrial machinery industries qualify for special tax treatment. This
treatment was introduced in 1961 and is due to come to an end in
1974.

In Spain, the formation of a new company by merger or take-over
qualifies for the following tax benefits:

- total exemption from the general tax on transfers of assets
  and legal acts based on a document (i.e. those necessary for
  the merger);
- total exemption from the general tax on income from capital
  in respect of the capital gains arising out of merger operations.

Table 1 summarises, by industry, the concentration operations
approved by the Government between 1959 and 1972.

In some cases association arrangements, as distinguished from
merger, may be facilitated. In France provisions exist to facilitate the formation of "groupements" and "sociétés conventionnées".
In Spain, where there is a particularly large number of small and
medium-sized firms, associations of enterprises enjoy substantial
tax advantages.

80

TABLE 1
SPAIN

GOVERNMENT-APPROVED CONCENTRATION OPERATIONS, BY INDUSTRY, 1959 - 1972

Industry	Number of firms before	Number of firms after	Type of Operation		Capital (ptas. million)
			Takeover	Merger	
Chemicals	74	32	28	2	221 478
Electrical engineering	140	48	35	3	61 909
Textiles	83	27	17	10	2 702
Food and beverages, tobacco	442	48	22	25	9 856
Transport equipment	59	22	17	5	14 860
Iron and steel	9	4	2	2	9 886
Non-ferrous metals	19	4	4	-	2 483
Metalworking	102	47	32	11	6 468
Building materials, glass and ceramics	80	32	23	9	7 697
Quarrying	26	9	5	4	6 894
Wood and cork products, and furniture	32	9	1	8	135
Paper and printing	32	14	11	3	3 963
Hides and skins	4	2	1	1	27
Miscellaneous	30	10	7	3	821
TOTAL	1 132	308	205	86	349 179

In the latter country two types of inter-firm co-operation are provided for. One involves the formation of a separate joint-stock company, and the other a less formal, temporary grouping organisation. In the former scheme the separate firms, whilst maintaining their individuality, pool their efforts in order to improve their production facilities, introduce new techniques or promote sales at home or abroad. The temporary grouping organisation, which is not a legal person, is a more flexible arrangement; it is set up by a simple agreement in the form of a public document entered in the Trade Register.

Apart from certain advantages with regard to local taxation, these companies or groups qualify for the following tax exemptions:

- 99 per cent of the general tax on transfers of assets and legal acts based on a document;
- 99 per cent of the turnover tax on transactions between the company or grouping organisation and the member firms;
- 99 per cent of the tax on the income from capital charged on profits distributed by the company or grouping organisation to the member firms;
- 95 per cent of the tax on income from capital charged on interest loans issued by Spanish enterprises and on loans arranged by Spanish enterprises with international organisations or foreign financial institutions.

Encouragement to utilise capital gains

Sales of assets frequently produce capital gains which are taxable in most countries. This may sometimes inhibit firms from making such capital gains manifest by turning them to account. Certain countries, therefore, have made their tax systems more flexible in this respect, apart from their policy of encouraging mergers.

In Germany, the mobility of production resources is encouraged by making it easier to transfer hidden reserves. Where the sale of durable goods or shares gives rise to the realisation of reserves, the acquisition of new assets out of these reserves may qualify for a special rate of depreciation allowance if the Ministry for Economic Affairs considers that the relevant transactions help towards the country's economic development. As a result of these regulations, introduced in 1965, the tax revenue forgone in 1971-1975 has been about DM.285 million a year.

In Sweden, certain operations may be wholly or partly exempted from taxation of capital gains if the payment of tax might inhibit structural adaptation. The main criteria taken into account by the authorities are the form of consideration, the effects of the transaction on employment, and the nationality of the acquiring company.

Exemption is most readily given where the consideration is an allotment of securities, when employment does not suffer and when only Swedish companies are involved. The utilisation by Swedish industry of this opportunity to avoid taxation of capital gains has so far been limited.

Up to 5 per cent of dividends received by Swedish companies may be deducted in similar conditions.

2. Financial instruments

The greater flexibility that is generally attainable through use of financial, as distinguished from fiscal, instruments has already been mentioned. This flexibility refers to the fuller scope possible in determining, for example, the recipients of aid and the amounts to be received on the basis of case-by-case consideration under the general criteria established, and the greater possibility that appears to exist, as a general rule at least, in ascertaining the effective use of aid in accordance with the policy objectives that gave rise to it. It may also be noted that the differentiated implementation of policies pursued by means of financial instruments is often facilitated by the association of such instruments with service-type measures (e.g. technical, managerial or other advisory activities), which by their nature are concerned with differentiated situations and needs.

The specific purposes for which financial incentives are used in the context of structural adaptation are very varied, including, inter alia, consultative services and studies preparatory to the undertaking of structural changes, the implementation of structural adaptation itself, including aids to merger or association, and the improvement of efficiency through the modernisation of plant and equipment, etc. It will be noted from the examples below that a major general objective to which these various types of adaptive behaviour are expected to contribute is that of adjustment to changing conditions of international competition.

Some country notes

Some countries rely on international competition to provide the stimulus for structural optimisation. In Australia the Government has recently been endeavouring to improve the allocation of resources by looking more critically at the question of tariff assistance. A review of the relatively high duty level tariff items which had not been examined for some time was commenced in 1971. In addition, in 1973, the Australian Government reduced all non revenue tariffs by 25 per cent. These moves have had the effect of stimulating further competition from overseas.

However, whilst these actions will no doubt result in better re-
source allocation, greater specialisation and ultimately a higher
standard of living, restructuring industry in this way raises a
number of immediate short-term problems. The Australian Government
in February 1973 established a special committee to advise on measures to facilitate the desired structural change in the economy.
The 25 per cent tariff out of July 1973 was introduced, however, before the committee's report was received and an interim adjustment
assistance programme was therefore introduced. In April 1974 details of the permanent programme were announced. Adjustment assistance programmes are relatively new in Australia and practical experience is being gained in administering the programme.

The stated aim of the structural adjustment assistance programme
is to promote and ease the process of desired change by providing
various incentives to industry. The Australian Government has argued
that if changes are desirable in the national interest, the nation
and not the individuals affected should meet the costs involved.

Some of the measures introduced are general in nature, whilst
others are devised for specific industries. Firms able to show that,
in spite of their efforts, they are badly hit by the structural
changes brought about by specified actions and that no existing provisions meet their case, can avail themselves of the following:

- grants covering consultancy services equal to 50 per cent of
  their cost up to a maximum of $10,000;
- loan guarantees;
- closure compensation (on a basis of 85 per cent of the difference between book value and realised value);
- special assistance for firms situated in non-metropolitan
  areas.

In Canada, the Federal authorities have taken steps to help
firms adapt to changes in the world trading environment arising out
of the Kennedy Round.

The General Adjustment Assistance Programme (G.A.A.P.) introduced in 1968 enables firms, on payment of a fee, to obtain loan insurance where they could not otherwise raise money on the financial
market. Grants are also provided to hire consultants, and direct
loans may be granted in special circumstances.

Applications have been approved in 121 cases; the resultant
increase in sales is estimated at $229,346,000, and the employment
increase at 5,554. Originally, small and medium-sized firms mainly
benefited from the programme but eligibility criteria were broadened
in 1973 and it is expected that increased utilisation will result.
Over 80 per cent of the guarantees have been granted to firms in the
following industries:

Electrical and electronic engineering	37 per cent
Clothing and textiles	29 per cent
Aerospace, marine and rail	15 per cent

Table 2 gives some further details for the last three years.

Table 2

CANADA

G.A.A.P. LOAN GUARANTEES GRANTED FROM 1971/72 TO 1973/74

	1971/72	1972/73	1973/74
Number of loan guarantees approved	32	23	23
Total amount (\$000's)	19 947	15 721	10 799
Average loan insurance (\$000's)	623	683	469

In 1970 a Programme to Enhance Productivity (P.E.P.) was launched providing government support for projects designed to increase productivity. Grants normally cover 50 per cent of the cost of a study up to a ceiling of \$50,000. It has been proposed to decentralise part of the administration to better assist small and medium-sized firms. Out of the 179 applications approved, 95 have been completed. The annual savings are estimated at \$30 million. Seventy per cent of the total amount went to the following industries:

- Clothing and textiles	26.4 per cent
- Materials	20.7 per cent
- Agric. fish and food prod.	12.1 per cent
- Electrical and electronic engineering	10.9 per cent

Table 3 gives some further information covering the last three years:

Table 3

CANADA

P.E.P. PROJECTS APPROVED 1971/72 - 1973/74

(In \$)

	1971/72	1972/73	1973/74
Number of projects approved	53	63	61
Funds committee	811 438	873 710	679 647
Average size of project	15 300	13 900	11 800
Funds expended	244 491	683 140	735 991

In France, loans from the FDES can be granted to industrial firms
in line with specific objectives. They are granted upon the advice of
specialised committees of the FDES management board. Certain loans can
also be granted upon the advice of the "Comité Interministériel pour
l'Aménagement des Structures Industrielles" (CIASI). This Committee,
established by an Order of 28th November, 1974, is responsible for
studying the situation of basically sound industrial enterprises
which, while adequately managed, have met with structural financial
difficulties. Loans granted in 1974 made it possible to continue
pilot operations launched in earlier years for restructuring industry. Firms in difficulties owing to the general economic situation
could also be helped. The main operations undertaken during the
three years from 1972 to 1974, as shown in Table 3A, came under the
heading of three types of sectoral plan and the restructuring of the
motor-vehicle industry (in 1974):

Table 3A

FRANCE

LOANS COMMITTED BY FDES FROM 1972 TO 1974

(Millions of francs)

Operations undertaken	1972		1973		1974	
	Number	Amount	Number	Amount	Number	Amount
Machinery Plan	5	12.5	8	50.4	3	16.5
Iron & Steel Plan	1	370.0	3	530.0	3	760.0
"Plan Calcul"	2	70.0	2	70.0	2	70.0
Decentralisation operations	9	28.8	5	18.0	2	4.0
Capital investment & conversion operations	2	8.0	11	215.0	14	77.4
Restructuring of motor-vehicle industry	–	–	–	–	2	1,450.0
Restructuring of industrial enter- prises (cases submitted to CIASI)	–	–	–	–	1	2.0
Total	19	489.3	29	883.4	27	2,379.9

In Norway, an Industrial Adjustment Fund was set up in 1963 to
help local firms adjust to the new conditions created when the
European Free Trade Association (E.F.T.A.) was set up. The grants
cover 50 per cent of the cost of each approved project and generally
continue for three years. In almost all cases the object has been to
assist mergers or group-formation. For 1973 the appropriation to the
fund totalled Kr.7 million.

The export promotion activities of the fund have now been de-
tached from it, and are covered by the Export Development Fund with
a current appropriation of Kr.9 million.

In Finland, since 1968, interest relief may be granted on Post
Office Bank loans to finance investment projects, with particular
consideration being given to projects involving production based on
new R & D activities and improvement of productivity and profitability
as well as to the international competitive situation of the industry;
implications with respect to reduction in energy consumption are also
taken into account. The loans cover up to 50 per cent of the total
cost and may be granted for a maximum of ten years. Repayments can
be deferred for up to 2 years and firms must pay at least 5 per cent
interest. The difference between the rate charged by Post Office
Bank (about 10 per cent) and that actually paid by the borrower is
met from budgetary funds. In practice interest relief over the last
two years has been 2 per cent.

The budgetary appropriation for this fund has been about Mks.20
million a year between 1969 and 1974.

3. Assistance by special public or semi-public bodies

This section deals with two approaches - long-term loans and
the acquisition of equity holdings - both through the agency of special public or semi-public bodies obtaining their funds both from
the State and from private investors. The two approaches may be used
separately or in combination. It should be noted that these institutions often play a "radar" role in seeking systematically to iden-
tify industrial development needs and opportunities, and in some
countries fulfill a very significant function in the implementation
of industrial policy.

Long-term loans

Many credit institutions with close government links play their
part in structural adjustment policy. In France there are the Caisse
des dépôts, Crédit foncier and Crédit national, in the United Kingdom
the Finance Corporation for Industry and the Industrial and Commercial
Finance Corporation, in Italy the Istituto di Credito Mobiliare and
Mediobanca, in Finland the mortgage bank, in Japan, the Japan
Development Bank, etc. The State helps by making special appropriations or contributions to such funds, by giving them precedence on
the capital market, providing guarantees for cash availabilities or
loan repayment and lastly giving interest relief in order to enable
them to lend on better terms than the ordinary market.

In Italy, for example, the Government has paid L.113,000 million
to the Istituto di Credito Mobiliare which finances loans to small

and medium-sized firms having adjustment difficulties. Under Act
No. 1470 of 18th December, 1961, such firms could borrow at a rate
of 3 per cent for a period of 15 years, if in a critical situation,
to enable them to adjust and to convert their production. A more
recent Act, passed in 1971, has extended this facility to all firms
irrespective of size; however, borrowing rates and periods depend
on location.(1) Fully-committed Government loans for this purpose
total L.40,000 million.

In Finland, the Mortgage Bank, a special credit institution,
will finance investment projects only if their value exceeds Mks.10
million, and then only on normal market terms. It requires the whole
of the loan to be secured by mortgage, its resources being mainly
borrowed.

Acquisition of equity holdings

Direct participation in industry through public or semi-public
bodies represents in some countries a significant instrument of
structural adaptation policy. There are indications that the resort
to this approach has been increasing in recent years along with the
emergence of increasingly active industrial policies and the growing
complexity of the problems to which such policies have been address-
ing themselves. Such participation has often been used to rationalise
or reorganise industries considered to be of key importance to the
national economy or to give an initial impetus to technologically advanced firms (frequently with the intention of withdrawing participation when self-sufficiency is attained) where risks are high and
return on investment may be expected only in a longer-term perspective. The public or semi-public bodies involved frequently are empowered to provide both equity and loan capital.

Set up in the form of a company with its share capital split
between the State and various banks, the role of the French Institute
for Industrial Development (I.D.I.) is to assist medium-sized firms
by subscribing for share or debentures (convertible or otherwise)
and by granting medium and long-term loans.

In Belgium, the Société Nationale d'Investissement is a corporation organised in the public interest (société anonyme d'intérêt
public) with state participation. Set up in 1962 it promotes the
formation, re-organisation and enlargement of industrial or commercial firms by acquiring shareholdings. Its particular object is
to support:

- dynamic firms that are too small to raise money on the
  capital market;

---

1) 3 per cent and 15 years in the south, 4 per cent and 15 years in
   the underprivileged North Centre areas, and 5 per cent and 10
   years elsewhere.

- innovating, strong or expanding firms, particularly in the advanced-technology industries;
- firms which could generate growth around them or contribute to economic growth generally, particularly in the development areas;
- firms capable of reaching "European" dimensions.

The S.N.I. also gives government guarantees to firms with real but not entirely risk-free prospects of recovery or firms whose activities involve a particularly high level of risk. Under the law dated 30th March, 1976, on the organisation of public economic initiative, the S.N.I. has been transformed into a public holding company. The S.N.I. can now, in addition to the tasks entrusted to it in the past and in the absence of private initiatives, create public companies, with an exclusively public ownership or a mixture of public and private ownership.

The Norwegian Industrial Fund is one of the most recent organisations of this type to have been instituted, having been in operation since 1st January, 1974. An allocation of Kr.75 million was earmarked for it in the 1972/73 budget. It is empowered to borrow up to Kr.300 million on the financial market, backed by government guarantee. The guarantees that it will be awarding will be covered in their turn by government guarantees up to a figure of Kr.200 million. It will be granting medium or long-term loans from its resources and will be acquiring holdings in order to finance industrial rationalisation and re-organisation.

The Spanish reply to the questionnaire states that the "National Institute for Industry is probably the most effective instrument available during recent years for implementing the country's industrial policy". This Institute was brought into being by an Act passed on 25th September, 1941. Its purpose is to "stimulate and finance in the service of the nation, the creation and revival of the country's industry, particularly where the firms concerned are involved in national defence or contributing to its economic independence". In these areas the object of the Institute is to make good any shortcomings in private initiative. Its management methods are the same as those used by all firms.

Its economic importance comes out clearly from Table 4.

Table 5 shows the situation as regards I.N.I. holdings at the end of 1972.

More generally, wholly or partially government-owned enterprises play an active role in implementing structural adaptation policies even when there is no co-ordination between their management and a central financial organisation such as the Italian E.N.I.

Table 4

SPAIN

ORIGIN AND SCALE OF I.N.I. INVESTMENT
DURING THE 5 YEARS 1968 - 1972

(In %)

Year	I.N.I. participation		Source of I.N.I. investment finance			
	in GFCF(1)	in industrial investment	State contributions	Self-financing	Financing loans	Pre-financing loans
1968	2.5	8.2	19.5	4.1	69.8	6.6
1969	2.7	8.7	18.1	3.0	72.6	6.3
1970	3.4	11.7	16.0	2.7	71.6	9.7
1971	1.7	6.3	21.6	3.3	65.3	9.8
1972	2.3	8.8	21.4	3.6	68.7	6.3

1) In 1972, Spanish gross fixed capital formation totalled
   Ptas.607,000 million.

Table 5

SPAIN

SHARE HOLDINGS BY I.N.I. (end 1972)

Extent of holding	Number of companies	Total capital (ptas million)	Average percentage holding
All share capital	14	15 279	100.0
Majority	31	68 105	82.1
50/50	2	4 776	59
Minority	11	23 182	18.2
Total	58	111 342	69.9

In France, public enterprises account for about 12 per cent of
added value, 13 per cent of manpower employed and 32 per cent of investment for all productive sectors excluding agriculture. Their
main public sources of finance are budgetary appropriations, cross-
subsidies and F.D.E.S. loans.

In Finland, public enterprise undertakings also occupy an important position in economic life. For some years the intention has
been to use them as an effective instrument of industrial policy.
The share of state-owned industrial companies in the turnover of all
industry amounted to 15.3 per cent in 1973. The State participates
in the financing of these companies principally by increasing the

share capital and providing guarantees on loans obtained in the domestic or foreign capital markets.

The annual increases in the share capital financed out of the State budget in recent years have been:

1969	Mks.107 million
1970	Mks.75 million
1971	Mks.180 million
1972	Mks.125 million
1973	Mks.91 million

Between 1962 and 1973 about three-quarters of the total amount involved went to the following industries:

Metals and metal working	50 per cent
Wood products	10 per cent
Electric power plants	12 per cent

4. Export promotion

While the measures included under this heading are not designed explicitly to act upon industrial structures - or at least not as their primary and immediate point of impact - they are closely linked to structural policy. The aim of export promotion policies converges with one of the major goals of structural policy: the improvement in the export performance of a country's industry. In a number of cases, in fact, export promotion forms an integral part of structural adaptation programmes addressed to given industrial sectors.

In certain countries such as Australia or Canada home markets are too small for full advantage to be taken of the economies of scale possible with mass production and governments therefore endeavour to help firms enlarge their markets by providing them with export incentives. A further effect of this is to diversify exports, largely made up of primary products.

In Australia, the Export Incentive Grant scheme was originally introduced in 1961 as a payroll tax rebate scheme designed, at a time of general slackness in the economy and pessimism in future balance of payments prospects, to encourage manufacturers to develop export markets. The scheme involved a rebate of payroll tax granted to an exporter to the extent of 10.5 per cent of the increase in his export sales over the average of the first three of the eight years preceding the year of export. Originally designed as a short-term measure, the payroll tax scheme was extended until the handing over of payroll tax measures to the States in 1971. Since that time the scheme has been operating as a system of direct grants to exporters. The estimated costs of this scheme are presented in Table 6.

Table 6

AUSTRALIA

ESTIMATED COSTS OF EXPORT INCENTIVE GRANT SCHEME

(1969/70 - 1973/74)

(In $ millions)

Export incentives	1969/1970	1970/71	1971/72	1972/73	1973/74
Grants	-	-	-	41	67
Payroll tax rebates	34	49	60	19	2

The Export Market Development Allowance was introduced in 1961 at the same time as the Incentive Grants Scheme. This measure also was designed to increase export activity by manufacturers and was not originally intended to become permanent. The concession was designed to allow a special rebate of eligible promotion expenditure over and above the deductions available under the income tax law. The maximum tax saving under this scheme (from normal and rebate deduction together) was limited to 87.5 cents in the dollar of eligible expenditure. It is estimated that this measure "cost" approximately $12 million and $24 million of forgone revenue in 1969/70 and 1973/74 respectively.

Both the grants incentive scheme and the development allowance were replaced in July 1974 by the Export Market Development Grants Scheme designed to run for five years. Under this scheme taxable grants are payable on export promotion expenditure in respect of any exports of substantially Australian origin.

With regard to export financing, the Australian Government established in 1956 an independent statutory authority (the Export Payments Insurance Corporation) designed to provide a specialised range of insurance and guarantee facilities against the risks of non-payment not normally available from commercial insurers. The Corporation has recently been incorporated as part of a larger organisation, the Export Finance and Insurance Corporation which is both an export financing agency and an export insurance agency.

In Canada, under the Programme for Export Market Development (P.E.M.D.) introduced in 1971, repayable contributions are provided towards certain travel and non-recurring expenses. The programme consists, at present, of 5 component sections, firms being encouraged to: participate in capital projects abroad, develop new markets, participate in trade fairs, invite foreign buyers to Canada, and to form export consortia.

It is estimated that the $4.3 million spent on the 1,901 projects approved should result in additional sales of $200 million. It is proposed to decentralise some of the administration in order to provide better assistance to small and medium-sized firms.

B. SECTORAL POLICIES

1. General survey

To a large extent, adaptation policies emerged in a sectoral context, as governments responded to needs or pressures as they arose in various parts of the industrial system. But increasingly, the attempt has been made to bring sectoral policies within a more integrated perspective concerned with the development of industry as a whole and, as one means to this end, to expand and intensify policy action directed to industry in general or large inter-sectoral portions thereof, such as small and medium-sized businesses; such policy action has been aimed, for example, at modernisation, technological innovation, improved management and labour efficiency. This more systematic attention to the viability of the whole industrial fabric was a response to the rapid and far-reaching changes in the environment of industrial activity and, to a significant extent, to the challenges and opportunities presented by international trade liberalisation as well as by the development and expansion of the European Community.

In some countries the evolution has been somewhat different from that sketched above: these are countries which have traditionally relied mainly on general economic policies and in which industrial policies, to the extent that they existed, already tended to be of a macro-industrial rather than sectoral character. In these countries, too, the rapid changes mentioned above have stimulated a more intense consideration of the role that industrial policies could play in promoting the structural adaptations which were becoming ever more clearly necessary; in at least one or two cases, this strengthened concern with industrial policy involved a greater emphasis on sectoral policies than was previously the case.

Whatever the historical evolution followed by given countries, however, and despite the great differences of approach that subsist, there seems to have been a general convergence towards a recognition that sectoral problems can be adequately understood only in the context of industry as a whole. This recognition is reflected in terms of actual policies, of course, to different degrees and in different ways. But this general development towards a more integrated perspective on sectoral problems should be kept in mind in reading the detailed accounts of specific sectoral policies below.

As for the types of industries which have been the object of sectoral policies, those noted in the country replies may for the sake of facilitating discussion, and despite the logical shortcomings of any such general categorisation, be considered under two general headings:

93

i) Certain traditional industries in which governments have
sought to promote adaptation to far-reaching economic and technological change, often involving the objective of significant restructuring and, in some cases, partial reconversion of activities; employment maintenance, often in a regional context, has usually been
an important concern of governments with regard to these industries.
Among the activities involved have been labour-intensive activities
in sectors such as textiles and clothing, footwear and leather products, which have had to face competition from low-cost production
in developing countries and have received assistance with a view,
e.g., to modernisation, restructuring and shifts in product lines.

In the general category of older industries which have sometimes been the object of assistance from the public authorities, one
may also mention iron and steel, where restructuring and rationalisation have been promoted by some governments, as well as shipbuilding.
Some elaboration of the rationale behind policies with respect to
shipbuilding may be in order, as this sector is mentioned by several
countries in some detail. Reorganisation of this industry before
the crisis of October 1973 was generally envisaged within a world
context of trade expansion, notably in the energy field, and involved technological reorientation, particularly the construction of
large tankers and specialised vessels. Since the energy crisis, the
conditions in which governments envisaged the reorganisation of the
industry have been fundamentally changed; a foreseen world excess
capacity in oil transport and shipbuilding beyond 1980 has now im-
pelled many governments to focus their policies on international co-
operation with a view to a reduction of production capacity.

ii) A rather heterogeneous group of mechanical and electrical
engineering industries (often including the manufacture of machine-
tools) which may be grouped together because they are considered,
for different reasons, to be important elements of modern economies.
These industries embrace both capital goods necessary to the functioning of a sophisticated economy and some consumer durables, in
particular automobiles. The reasons why governments have been im-
pelled to provide assistance to these sectors include the desire to
promote modernisation and technological innovation, and sometimes to
remedy structural deficiencies, in order to create or maintain efficient production for domestic use and/or to improve competitivity
in international markets. It may be added, with reference to automobiles, that in some countries this sector has particular importance
in the economy as a consumer of materials, as a sub-contractor to
other industries and as a source of employment.

Cutting across the types of sectors involved, the ways in which
sectoral policies are formulated and implemented are highly variable
and may have considerable significance with respect to the impact of

the sectorally oriented measures and programmes on the whole complex
of policies affecting industry. In order to reflect the country
diversity in this respect, as well as to describe policies which are
conceived for and applied to such and such a sector individually, the
detailed country rates below will give examples, first, of certain
policy frameworks applicable to a plurality of sectors, and then of
individual sector policies. The examples of individual sector policies will be organised according to the two general sectoral types
described above and also, in two brief final sections, according to
two special objectives: i.e., sectoral policies to turn natural
resources to account and reorganising sectors specifically in the
interest of consumers.

2. Examples of pluri-sectoral policy frameworks

Specific action in the framework of general legislation

In the United Kingdom, alongside regional policy in which sectoral aspects are important, Section 8 of the Industry Act 1972 provides for assistance to be given where this is likely to benefit the
economy of any part of the United Kingdom and is in the national
interest. Assistance under Section 8 may take a variety of forms,
including loans, guarantees, grants and share-participations. During
1974/75, 26 applications under this Section were considered, of which
8 were withdrawn and 10 approved. Examples of the type of assistance
provided were:

1. Kearney and Trecker Ltd. received during 1973/74 £1.45 million
   (in the form of a £0.9 million loan and £0.5 million preference shares) to acquire Marwin Machine Tools Ltd. and so
   form a competitive machine-tool production unit. As part of
   a financial reconstruction in 1974 the Government made
   available up to £3.5 million (mainly preference shares) as
   needed to provide essential capital. At the same time, a
   loan of £0.9 million was capitalised in the form of preference
   shares.
2. To strengthen the British motor-cycle industry, assistance
   was given in 1973/74 to establish a new company, Norton
   Villiers Triumph Ltd., embracing the motor-cycle interests
   of BSA Ltd. and Manganese Bronze Holding Ltd. The assistance
   was by acquisition of preference shares in the new company
   and amounted to £4.8 million, of which £1.3 million would be
   convertible in equity. During 1974, a guarantee under
   Section 8 of up to £8 million for export stock finance was
   provided.

In 1975 a general scheme was introduced on a temporary basis for bringing forward investment projects that had been deferred during the recession.

The 1968 Industrial Expansion Act in the United Kingdom had authorised the Government to grant financial assistance for investment projects designed to improve the competitive situation of a firm or industry. For example, Anglesey Aluminium Ltd. and British Aluminium Company Ltd. received loans (£33 and £30 million respectively) at 7 per cent repayable over 30 years to assist the construction of smelters at Holyhead and Ivergordon. This Act also empowered the Government to make a grant of £13.5 million to International Computers Limited when it was formed and to acquire 10 per cent of its share capital. Also under this Act special appropriations were allocated to certain projects. For example, under this Act (followed by the Concorde Aircraft Act 1973 which raised the financial limits of the assistance allowed) the construction of Concorde could be aided by the provision of £100 million (which could be increased later to £125 million). Another example is the £24 million loan to the Cunard Company to assist the construction and introduction service of the Queen Elizabeth II. The Industry Act 1972 repealed the power to support industrial investment schemes, although support could still be provided for schemes (e.g. aluminium smelters) already in being.

A programme covering several sectors

In Sweden, a decision was taken in 1971 to provide financial assistance for the textile and clothing industries but the importance of the investment reserve should not be forgotten and particularly the special releases for firms in a specific region or industry. In 1972 a sectoral assistance programme was introduced for a three-year trial period under the control of the National Industry Board. There are two main sides to this programme; grants offered to firms so that they may take expert advice with regard to restructuring problems, and guarantees and loans at market rates, sometimes accompanied by deferred repayment facilities or even, in some exceptional cases, temporary waives of interest for three years, are granted for a period of ten years or, more rarely, for 15 years, by A.B. Strukturgaranti, a new State-owned company. Lastly, special efforts have been made to develop exports from assisted industries by grants, guarantees and advice from specialists in international trade.

Apart from the textile and clothing industries, the main sectors to have benefited from this programme are the hosiery, footwear, furniture and glass industries. From 1974 on, the mechanical engineering industry has also qualified.

<u>Sectoral assistance under differently oriented programme types</u>

<u>Spain</u> offers a typical example of this type of sectoral assistance. Each of its schemes has its own purpose and is designed to solve a problem common to a whole industry. There are:

- sectoral restructuring schemes;
- preferential sectors;
- "concerted actions".

Sectoral restructuring schemes for the textile industries (cotton, wool and jute), the national refrigeration network, and flour production were all introduced in 1960 and have been maintained since that date. Their object is to stimulate the formation of competitive-sized production units by the takeover or elimination of marginal units. Where capacities are extended, preference in obtaining official loans(1) distributed by the Industrial Credit Bank is added to the facilities (substantial tax reductions) granted to sectors designated as "preferential interest sectors". Compensation is paid where production capacities have to be reduced.

For the woollen textiles industry, only one programme has been implemented with limited results, mainly because of over-contraction. But with the cotton textiles scheme, 70 per cent of the targets have been reached in the case of spinning and practically 100 per cent in the case of weaving, production capacities being used to about 90 per cent.

The provisions concerning <u>preferential sectors</u>, introduced in 1965 and since then extended to various other activities, are generally aimed at meeting the need to assist development in industries producing mainly intermediate goods.(2)

For each industry, the economic and social objectives to be reached are first established, together with the conditions necessary to qualify for the benefits to be granted, which are the same as for preferential interest industries plus priority in obtaining official loans.

<u>Concerted actions</u> stem from the need to restructure and gear up to international competition standard certain industries(3) regarded

---

1) Generally granted to firms with a share capital of under Ptas.500 million, and not exceeding 70 per cent of the total investment project, at a rate varying from 6 to 7 per cent depending on the period of the loan.

2)
Ethylene and polyethylene	Decree of 1-4-1965
Integrated steel works	Decree of 17-4-1969
Chemical monomers and polymers	Decree of 23-12-1971
Private cars	Decree of 23-12-1972
Sulphuric acid from pyrites	Decree of 5-4-1973
Firms supplying to the motor industry	Decree of 28-2-1974

3)
Iron and steel	Ministerial Order of 22-8-1964
Preserved vegetables	Ministerial Order of 22-8-1964
Leather	Ministerial Order of 22-8-1964
Paper	Ministerial Order of 17-7-1965
Shipbuilding	Ministerial Order of 26-7-1967

as particularly important because of their impact on the industrial economy or their export potential. The economic and social objectives to be achieved are established for each industry together with the conditions to be fulfilled by those firms signing the agreement. Apart from the general advantages granted to preferential interest industries and their priority in obtaining official credit, each agreement includes special benefits for the signatory firms. In industries where large-scale firms predominate (iron and steel and shipbuilding) results of concerted actions have been very satisfactory. They appear to have been less successful in industries where small and medium-sized firms are still very numerous (paper, leather, and preserved vegetables) because of the difficulty of organising concertation with a large number of members.

Table 7 sums up the situation at the end of 1972 for concerted actions in the manufacturing industries.

3. Examples of individual schemes

Older or traditional industries

In Australia, competition from low cost imports in a section of the apparel industry (knitted shirts and some knitted outerwear) led to an inquiry by the Tariff Board which, in 1971, recommended a lowering of duties on the goods concerned. However, because these sectors of the apparel industry employed a significant number of people, the Government took steps by way of temporary import licensing to provide the industry with time to restructure its activities. After the breakdown of negotiations on the limitation of imports from the three main supplying developing countries, tariff quotas were introduced to replace the quantitative restrictions. The tariff quotas were removed in February 1974. This move, along with the 25 per cent tariff cut of July 1973 resulted in a further substantial growth in imports of textiles and apparel goods during 1974. Following reports from the Textiles Authority, Australia has taken action to stabilise the situation by initiating voluntary restraint arrangements in terms of the GATT Textiles Arrangement and by the introduction of a system of tariff quotas.

For the footwear industry, the Australian Government in 1966 adopted a Tariff Board recommendation which said that two rates - a general rate of 45 per cent and a preferential rate of 25 per cent - or alternative specific rates, would provide adequate long term protection for efficient local manufacturers whilst also providing a sound basis for the industry to continue its restructuring. The alternative specific duties were recommended to provide extra assistance to non-leather footwear manufacturers who were developing more competitive forms of production and were incurring substantial cost

TABLE 7

SPAIN

CONCERTED ACTIONS IN THE MANUFACTURING INDUSTRIES—SITUATION AT END 1972

	Number of firms signing agreement	Share in Industry's total output (in %)	Value of investment projects provided for in the agreements	Official credit granted	Official credit formally made available	
					Used	Unused
			Million pesetas			
Steel industry	17	59	37 556	25 034,2	21 043,2	3 231,2
Leather	80	4	950	581,2	453,8	76,3
Preserved vegetables	65	20	2 304	768,1	684,9	73,2
Paper	26	33	6 650	1 634,4	1 458,7	114,9
Shipbuilding	4	90	5 717	2 827,0	632,5	2 194,5

disadvantages by using certain costly local materials. In 1970, the
Tariff Board reported that the readjustment and rationalisation of
the footwear industry had continued with the more viable sections of
the industry increasing their sales and profitability. It recommended
the phasing down of the specific rates over a five year period. However, by 1974 a similar situation to that in apparel and textiles
had arisen. Imports of all types of footwear increased during
1973/74 by 70 per cent over the previous year. Following an independent inquiry by the Temporary Assistance Authority, Australia again
found it necessary to introduce temporary import restrictions in the
form of quotas to moderate the rate of change.

The strategy adopted by Canada in 1970 in the textiles scheme
was based on recognition of the fact that it was difficult to compete
with the developing countries, which had lower production costs, in
day-to-day and medium quality articles. The answer was to concentrate
on high-quality products for Canadian consumers and typically
Canadian-style products for export. Apart from the assistance given
to firms for structural adaptation, a vigorous promotional policy
was put into effect.

Industry restrictions was assisted in five main ways by applying
the national programmes(1) purpose-modified in some cases:

- Financial support
- Promotional support (for exports)
- Manpower development and adjustment
- Development and productivity centres
- Fashion design assistance.

Insured loans totalling $20 million were received by thirty-
eight firms. In addition eleven received consulting grants, totalling
$85,000. Twenty-five to thirty firms have received assistance each
year for their R & D activities and $2.4 million was spent by the
Federal Government to assist them in commercialising R & D results.
The Government also spent $163,000 to support 65 companies in their
export efforts.

The results of this strategy seem to have been positive since,
between 1970 and 1972, clothing exports went up by 26 per cent from
$73 million to $92 million and textile exports reached a figure of
$120 million, an increase of 16 per cent over the same period.

A special effort has been made to raise the level of skill in
the industry. Also, pre-retirement benefits are provided for workers
made redundant by industry restructuring. 148 applications have
been allowed with payments of $520,000.

---

1) General Adjustment Assistance Program - G.A.A.P.
   Industrial Research and Development Incentives Act - I.R.D.I.A.
   Program for the Advancement of Industry Technology - P.A.I.T.
   Program for Export Market Development - P.E.M.D.

Joint industry/government task forces have been examining the best means of ensuring that the industry obtains maximum advantage from new products and the latest developments in production processes and techniques.

In view of the importance of artistic skills for the development of the textile and clothing industry, the Federal Government spent about $190,000 on the training and employment of fashion designers capable of giving distinction originality to national merchandise.

Central to commercial policy was the setting up of the Textile and Clothing Board which determines whether certain imports threaten Canadian production and when necessary, informs the Goverment which may impose quantitative restrictions. Also, tariffs have been altered in order to remove certain anomalies whereby tariffs on constituent materials were higher than the end-product. Lastly, Canada is actively involved in the G.A.T.T. negotiations aimed at reducing barriers to international trade in textile products.

The special situation(1) of the footwear and tanning industries called for a strategy based mainly on the formation of larger production units capable of establishing themselves on both home and foreign markets. Action in this case takes three forms: productivity improvement, marketing practices and commercial policy.

As regards productivity improvement, it is a matter of employing consultancy firms and taking advice with regard to introducing restructuring programmes. Firms received grants of up to 80 per cent of the cost of consultant services and loans to help finance implementation costs. Inter-firm comparisons are used to test the effectiveness of the measures themselves and of their application so that the most suitable may be selected and put into general use. At the same time efforts were made by the Department of Manpower and Immigration and the organisations concerned to upgrade manpower skills at all levels.

"Marketing Practices" includes the setting up of a design centre working on the style, shape and colour of products to be offered on home and foreign markets.

Commercial policy is designed to protect the home industry against unfair competition and to reduce duty on materials used in local products.

In Italy, the act of 1st December, 1971 authorises an ad hoc inter-ministerial policy committee to grant loans at a rate of 4 per cent for a maximum period of 15 years for structural adaptation, reorganisation and conversion in the textile industry. Small and medium-sized firms have preferential treatment in that the amount that can be borrowed is inversely proportional to the total project

_____

1) The footwear industry consists of 175 establishments employing 18,000 people; there are 30 tanneries with 2,900 employees.

figure.(1) The Government has spent L.210,000 million in interest
reliefs for these loans financed by medium-term credit institutes.
In 1972 it was decided to extend the measure to other industries.

Special mention should be made here of an approach to the restructuring or adaptation of certain sectors in France, involving
the financing by parafiscal taxes of special sectoral committees
created for the purpose and managed by the industry concerned. For
example, CIRIT (Comité Interprofessionel de Rénovation de l'Industrie
Textile) is financed by a parafiscal tax levied on the added value
of textiles manufactured in France or imported from countries outside the EEC.

In the United Kingdom a scheme of assistance for the wool textile industry was introduced under Section 8 of the Industry Act 1972,
in July 1973. The scheme was designed to encourage on the one hand
greater efficiency through modernisation of plant and rationalisation
of production of facilities, and on the other elimination of surplus
capacity and a reduction of the number of firms in the industry.
Assistance in the form of grants or loans at concessionary rates was
available under the scheme to firms proposing projects aimed at these
objectives. The scheme closed for applications at the end of 1975.

Three further sectoral schemes aimed at modernisation and rationalisation were introduced in the second half of 1975. These were
for the Ferrous Foundry, Machine Tools and Clothing Industries.

In Australia, where it was felt that protecting the shipbuilding
industry by tariffs could have disadvantages for local users (e.g.
fishing fleets and coastal shipping service clients), a special measure was introduced in order to lower the prices of vessels built by
Australian shipyards. A ban on imports of ships of over 200 tons
gross was coupled with a system of subsidies of up to 45 per cent of
the cost of building vessels in Australia. Taken together, these
measures provided protection of a high order, and involved total
subsidy payments of $30.7 million in 1972/73 compared with $13.4 million in 1971/72. The Government in 1973 decided to bring assistance
to shipbuilders more in line with assistance available to other
areas of manufacturing industry. Coverage was extended to include
ships over 150 tons gross, fishing vessels over 21 metres in length

---

1) 70 per cent up to L.500 million, 60 per cent for 500 - 3,000
   million and 50 per cent for 3-6,000 million.

and Australian flag vessels in international trade. It was decided
to phase-down the maximum subsidy by 30th December 1980 from 45 to
25 per cent. The bounty is assessed on the lowest acceptable
Australian tender. The ban on imports continues but is lifted where
the price of a foreign ship is lower than that quoted by the
Australian shipyard less the subsidy. At the present time the authorities are considering whether loans at concessionary rates might
be made available in line with the OECD understanding.

In Canada, the Shipbuilding Temporary Assistance Programme
(S.T.A.P.) was introduced at the end of 1970 in order to maintain
employment levels pending recovery in home demand. Grants of up to
17 per cent of approved costs are awarded for ships contracted for
prior to 31st March, 1975 and completed before 31st October, 1978.

Under the Ship Construction Subsidy Regulation, which has been
in force since 1961, ships built for Canadian registry received a
grant of 17 or 35 per cent of their cost depending on whether they
are to be used for sea transport or for fishing. Originally these
rates were 40 and 50 per cent respectively.

Table 8 gives some further information for this industry.

Table 8

CANADA

SHIPBUILDING - STAP AND SCSR FIGURES

	1968-69 or 1968(1)	1969-70 1969	1970-71 1970	1971-72 1971	1972-73 1972
Total amount of STAP and SCSR grants ($ millions)	22.3	14.2	13.7	10.2	31.5
Numbers employed in industry	15,660	15,183	13,790	13,259	14,647
Value of shipbuilding ($ millions) not in-cluding repairs	154.0	131.3	91.6	119.6	231.5

1) The amount of subsidies is given for the fiscal year and the remainder of the information per calendar year.

In France, shipbuilding aids were instituted by law in 1951.
They may be granted to commercial ships of more than 150 tons built
in France, regardless of the purchaser's nationality. Two types of
aid may be distinguished: -the "basic grant", which is proportional
to the contract price for the vessel. The rate has been substantially
reduced since 1969, when it still stood at 10 per cent; in 1974 it
had fallen to 2 per cent for small vessels and to 0.5 per cent for
larger ships;- the "price guarantee", enabling shipyards to offer

their customers terms in line with those of competing foreign shipyards. The State assumes responsibility for any price rise beyond a
certain level between the placing of an order and delivery. The
price guarantee is applicable to large and medium-sized vessels.
The duration of the guarantee, which was nearly five years in 1969,
has been reduced to three or two years, depending on the size of the
ship. The amount of the rise which the shipyard must bear was gradually increased from 3 per cent in 1969 to over 5 per cent in 1974.
Small vessels have occasionally benefited from the price guarantee.
In this event it is for a two-year period and thresholds approximat-
ing those of the major shipyards are applied. From 1972 to 1974 programme authorisations under this heading were as follows: Frs.654.7
million in 1972; Frs.710.6 million in 1973 and Frs.800.2 million in
1974.

Sustaining and developing modern industries

In Canada, as part of the Machinery Program which was set up in
1968 as a result of the Kennedy Round, the authorities are attempting
to reconcile two objectives: to avoid penalising industry as a whole
by forcing it to buy home-produced machine tools at prices sometimes
higher than foreign products, and at the same time to expand production of machine tools in Canada. Under this pragmatic policy,
Canadian machine tool manufacturers are being encouraged to improve
their productivity and assisted in publicising their products at
home and abroad. But for requirements that the home industry could
not supply at reasonable cost, users are not prevented from obtaining
the most efficient machines since they are allowed to import them
duty-free. In recent years, exemptions from customs duty have totalled the amounts (in $ million) shown in Table 9.

Table 9

CANADIAN MACHINERY PROGRAM:

Exemptions from customs duty

($ 000,000)

1968	1969	1970	1971	1972	1973
45.0	60.0	75.0	78.0	93.0	110.0

Each year, a survey is made to determine firms' needs and they
are provided with an inventory of products available from Canadian
manufacturers and assistance is given to firms using home-built
machine tools.

In Australia, the relatively high level of protection required
by the machine tool industry has led the authorities to pay a

production bounty to Australian machine tool manufacturers so that a nucleus of an industry will be maintained without excessive cost to users of Australian built machine tools. The maximum grant is equivalent to one third of the factory cost of the machine but the actual amount of the bounty paid in each case depends upon the extent of the Australian content.

The Australian Government also pays a bounty to Australian manufacturers of agricultural tractors to reduce the price of tractors sold to farmers in accordance with the Government's wishes that "users of tractors should have access to tractors at prices which are not increased by any protective measures". The grant is paid only in respect of production and sales on the home market, the ceiling varying from $1,040 to $1,560 according to the power of the tractor, (15kW and above), and the size of the grant made depending on the proportion of Australian content in the finished product. Whilst the question of future grants is under review, the current arrangements will continue until the end of 1976. Total bounty payments in 1972/73 were $2.8 million and in 1973/74, $3.7 million.

For the motor and related industries, government policy is to endeavour to increase the extent to which national industry is involved in the manufacture or assembly of vehicles used in the country.

In Canada, the cornerstone for this policy was laid in 1965 and is the Canada-United States Automotive Agreement under which motor vehicles and parts may cross the border duty free. Having regard to the differences in size, strength and degree of development of the automotive industry in the two countries, it was agreed that sales by Canadian manufacturers should account for at least 75 per cent (or the corresponding percentage in 1964) of total Canadian sales and that the Canadian content (value added) in vehicles produced in Canada must be no less than the absolute dollar amount achieved in 1964. Similar provisions are available to other countries and Toyota and Volvo have taken advantage of them.

The automotive Adjustment Assistance Program[1] was set up in 1965 to provide financial assistance to Canadian manufacturers of motor parts. By 16th May 1974 loans totalling $115.7 million had been granted (committed funds), with a current outstanding loan balance of about $40 million. 120 applications had been approved and it is estimated that some 5,000 new jobs have been created. Since 1964, vehicle assembly in Canada has increased by 135 per cent, parts manufacture by 258 per cent, and the Canadian market for North American vehicles has increased by 38 per cent.

The Australian motor vehicle industry, in the late 1950's was assisted by tariffs set at a level designed to encourage local

1) Since merged with the General Adjustment Assistance Program.

component manufacture. Where gaps existed in local capacity however, duty free by-law entry for components was available. With the removal of import licensing in 1960, motor vehicle builders tended to revert to imported components. By the mid 1960's the Government using a series of local content plans acted to relate the availability of duty concessions under by-law to commitments by manufacturers to increase local content. The first Plan was introduced by the Government in 1965. It required manufacturers to achieve a 95 per cent local content within five years in return for duty free admission of all residual components. Two low local content Plans with restricted by-laws were also introduced. Between 1966 and 1971 the Plans were amended four times. In 1971 it was decided to phase out the low local content Plans to overcome problems of fragmentation in the light car market.

Recent developments in the Australian motor vehicle industry flow from new rules and objectives laid down by the Government in 1973. These objectives have been incorporated in the current policy for the motor vehicle industry which is built around a single 85 per cent local content plan which is on a company average basis rather than the previous model basis. The Plan, which is to operate for ten years, will be supported by a tariff of 35 per cent on completely built up (CBU) imports and 25 per cent on completely knocked down (CKD) imports. However, when CBU imports exceed 20 per cent of total new passenger vehicle registrations, these tariffs are to increase by 10 percentage points to 45 per cent and 35 per cent respectively.

In France some industries may be noted as receiving specific forms of assistance from the public authorities. The State grants various types of specific aid to the aircraft manufacturing sector in order to promote the construction of new aircraft or equipment. Such intervention is justified on the grounds that this is an advanced sector with a substantial technological spin-off, while one subject to heavy international competition. Aids are of four main types: one consists in furthering the development and mass production of new aircraft; a second in helping to launch certain kinds of equipment; a third specific aid may be granted to facilitate the marketing abroad of aircraft equipment; lastly the State grants loans to the SNIAS and SNECMA for financing the Concorde construction programme.

From 1972 to 1974 operations carried out under the heading of these aids were as follows:

- Aids for developing new aircraft:

(Millions of francs)

Major aircraft programmes	Programme authorisations issued		
	1972	1973	1974
Airbus (development and derived versions)	302.0	289.6	245.9
Motorization (Airbus and CFM 56)	16.0	45.2	119.0
Mercure (additional development)	152.0	98.0	11.4
Concorde	448.2	1,060.4	492.5
Miscellaneous equipment	4.3	2.6	
Total	922.5	1,495.8	868.8

- Aids for launching aircraft equipment and complex defence equipment: annual allocation from 1972 to 1974 of Frs.47 million.
- State contribution to marketing effort: programme authorisations: Frs.2.4 million in 1972; Frs.3.3 million in 1973 and Frs.3.9 million in 1974.
- Loans to the SNIAS and SNECMA: as at 31st December, 1974 Frs.715 million.
- Aids to computer and electronics industries.

A. The 'Plan Calcul'

The purpose of this aid is to promote the growth of computer research. It is granted in the form of research contracts, which are intended to further study and research programmes of the CII, French manufacturers of peripheral equipment and data-processing consultant services. Aid granted to the CII under the Plan Calcul is provided for by an agreement signed in 1971. From 1971 to 1973 all objectives assigned to the CII under the agreement were achieved. The company's turnover then rapidly increased, and in July 1973 it concluded an agreement for technical, industrial and commercial co-operation with the Siemens Company in Germany and Philips Company in the Netherlands (Unidata agreements). In 1974, however, the activity of the CII was adversely affected by the market's cyclical decline, by difficulties met with in implementing the Unidata agreements and by relations with its private shareholders. For these reasons a re-organisation plan was first investigated, then announced by the Government in May 1975. From 1972 to 1974 programme authorisations amounted to Frs.261 million, Frs.220 million and Frs.413 million respectively for those years.

B. Components Plan and Civil Professional Electronics Plan

Two projects are financed under this heading: a Components Plan, governed by the provisions of the so-called micro-electronics agreement signed in June 1968 by the Government and the profession; and a Civil Professional Electronics Plan, put into force in 1971 for providing aid to the French professional electronics industry in the form of research contracts. Programme authorisations have been as follows: Frs.15 million in 1972, Frs.86.5 million in 1973 and Frs.29 million in 1974.

Mention may be made of aid to the petroleum industry. Aids allocated from the Oil Support Fund were created in 1950. The Fund is the instrument used by the Government to develop oil research and production. Its resources are obtained from charges included in the prices for petroleum products. Action is of two kinds: through grants to the ERAP or through various types of assistance, as aid for promoting petroleum research in the seabed. Between 1972 and 1974 the Fund allocated Frs.230 million to the ERAP in 1972 and Frs.200 million in 1973.

These allocations find their justification in the necessity to allow the public establishment to pursue the diversification of petroleum research which the Government has requested it to undertake after the loss of assets located in Algeria. The other interventions of the Oil Support Fund are intended to assist in the financing of research and development of new technologies in the field of prospecting and exploiting petroleum in the seabed.

Between 1972 and 1974 these interventions have evolved as follows:

(Millions of francs)

	1972	1973	1974
Funds allocated	11.6	16.7	17.3

In France, the State can give assistance to the film industry with the object of allowing film production or distribution enterprises to remain in business. This assistance is financed mainly by the proceeds of the special tax levied on top of the price of admission to cinemas. Financial support for this sector can take different forms. Total disbursements rose from Frs.126.1 million in 1972 to Frs.147.6 million in 1973 and Frs.178.2 million in 1974. Repayments vary from year to year, and from 1972 to 1974 did not exceed 1.70 per cent of total disbursements.

Mention should also be made of two types of assistance which are connected with related economic activities: assistance for printing equipment and assistance for manufacturers of newsprint. Assistance for printing equipment. The newspaper enterprises receive assistance intended to facilitate the purchase of printing materials both with the objective of modernising equipment and for tax reasons. Printing plant was in fact neither renewed nor maintained during the 1939-1945 War. Moreover, up until 1955 the vast majority of newspaper enterprises were sequestrated and then managed by the SNEP, and their investment had, therefore, reached only a very modest level. Since, moreover, the press is exempt from VAT for the sale of newspapers, the enterprises are not able to recover tax paid on their investment. Assistance consists of a 14 per cent reimbursement on the purchase of printing equipment. It is granted to enterprises which set or print newspapers and periodicals included in a list drawn up by the joint press committee. It can also be extended to press agencies, photo-engraving, selling and mailing enterprises. Since 1969, the subsidy has also been granted to print shops whose VAT exempted income is greater than their income from jobbing printing. This aid is chargeable to the general services budget of the Prime Minister. Credits under this heading amounted to Frs.8.6 million in 1972, Frs.10.0 million in 1973 and Frs.6.4 million in 1974. Assistance for manufacturers of newsprint. Under the regulations applying to newsprint established in 1971, manufacturers of newsprint can receive official aid intended to offset the handicap borne by the national industry as regards supplies of wood. This aid comes under the budget for industry and research. Assistance disbursed under the press-papermills protocol of 1971 was calculated on the basis of a gradual reduction in the proportion of French paper in supplies to the press, and was indexed on the international price of paper so as to maintain a constant level of protection for French paper. The increase in the Government subsidy in 1974 was due to the abrupt rise in the international price from that date on. Under these circumstances, the assistance given is designed to ensure competitiveness and to facilitate the modernisation of enterprises manufacturing newsprint. It is allocated via the Caisse Générale de Péréquation de la Papeterie on presentation of a programme of which it has been informed by the Syndicat des Fabricants de Papier Journal. Credits granted under this heading amounted to Frs.14.8 million in 1972, Frs.13.9 million in 1973 and Frs.19.3 million in 1974.

Sectoral assistance in order to turn natural resources to account

Certain countries take steps to promote industries which exploit resources in which they are especially rich.

Canada, for example, produces large quantities of sulphur and is endeavouring to increase its share of the market, develop new processes in order to increase world consumption and obtain a better

price on the international market. Jointly with industry, the
Federal and Alberta governments have therefore set up the Sulphur
Development Institute of Canada (SUDIC), which is studying new applications, the various problems arising in transportation and handling,
and ways of improving productivity. The Institute receives a grant
from public funds.

In France, the agricultural and food industries can receive
three types of aid from the Ministry of Agriculture depending upon
the sector to which they belong:

- loans can be granted to saw-mills from the resources of the
  Fonds Forestier National;
- subsidies can be awarded under the heading of tuberculosis
  prevention;
- grants can be extended to enterprises in order to facilitate
  their investment.

To encourage the modernisation of saw-mills, loans can be
granted from the resources of the special Treasury account, the
"Fonds Forestier National". Between 1972 and 1974, the total volume
of loans increased from Frs.5,654 million in 1972 to Frs.13,489 million in 1973 and Frs.16,134 million in 1974.

In 1973 certain private bodies received subsidies under the
heading of tuberculosis prevention for the purchase of apparatus with
which to disinfect animal accommodation. The amount is in principle
restricted to 15 per cent of the cost of the equipment, and can be
varied according to requirements.

The "Primes d'Orientation Agricole" (POA) (agricultural orientation grants) are allocated to private or co-operative enterprises
on a selective basis as a means of encouraging them to pursue their
development along the lines laid down in the Plan. They take the
form of capital subsidies paid out of the appropriations of the agriculture budget.

In allocating this aid, priority is given to enterprises which
are making an effort to expand on foreign markets, which are restructuring or which contribute to regional development. Special
attention is still being given to the co-operative sector, which has
received almost half of the aid extended to the processing industries,
while it has been responsible for approximately 25 per cent of investment by the whole of the agricultural and food industry. 217
subsidies were granted in 1974, totalling Frs.159,316 million and
corresponding to investment worth Frs.1,116,507 million.

Restructuring a sector specifically in the interest of consumers

Where protection has been given for a long period to industries producing major consumer goods, the need to rationalise these industries has become increasingly apparent. Sheltered from international competition, many firms offer products in great variety but at a high price. Public opinion, well-informed through modern mass media, sometimes protests at the differences caused by this bad allocation of resources.

The Tariff Review Program undertaken by the <u>Australian</u> Government is expected to facilitate the availability to consumers of a wide range of cheaper commodities. This point was underlined by the Prime Minister in 1973 when, while announcing a lowering of the electronics industry tariff rates, he said that this move would provide the Australian consumer with a wide range of cheaper electronic consumer goods.

In <u>Canada</u>, the Pharmaceutical Industry Development Assistance Program (PIDA) was created to assist the process of concentration necessary to reduce the price of drugs. Loans at close to commercial interest rates have been granted to most eligible companies. PIDA is authorised to lend $2 million and has $800,000 in loans outstanding. The objectives set would appear to have been attained.

Chapter 6

STRUCTURAL ADAPTATION AND MANPOWER

Change is inherent in economic growth and affects the labour market by modifying the location and nature of jobs as well as the level of skills required. The process of adjustment must be continuous if the distribution of the labour force by region, sector and level and type of training is to meet the requirements of a continuously changing production system. Lack of flexibility in this area could have an adverse effect on the basic equilibria of growth.

Thus, most governments are trying, in the framework of their economic and social policy, to match the supply of labour to demand. This means, for one thing, listing out requirements and availabilities and passing on the information to those concerned - employers and employees. In France, for example, the Agence Nationale pour l'Emploi /National Employment Agency/ fulfills this function. Then there are measures aimed at stimulating development in employment opportunities and in the supply of manpower. Encouraging firms to move or assisting an industry to restructure are ways of developing employment opportunities, and measures designed to promote the geographical or occupational mobility of manpower reflect a desire to influence labour supply.

As far as the worker is concerned, change implies a major risk: that of losing his job and hence his livelihood. Here there are two possible policies. Governments can either compensate in the form of unemployment benefit or guaranteed incomes, or else take preventive action by encouraging geographical and occupational mobility of manpower so that it corresponds to the changing requirements.

On the basis of the present enquiry, three major objectives for manpower adjustment policies may be noted: guaranteed incomes, occupational mobility and geographical mobility. Some countries have also referred to other purposes, the aim generally being to facilitate access to employment for under-privileged persons or groups such as the handicapped or the aged.

Before each of these objectives is examined in detail, the following table outlining the receipts and expenditures of the

German Federal Employment Bureau(1) will help to illustrate the various types of action currently undertaken. (See Table 10.)

A. OCCUPATIONAL MOBILITY

This is a means of matching skills to the nature of the jobs to be filled - which changes with time.

Low earnings and increasing mechanisation are driving workers out of agriculture into other jobs for which they are frequently not qualified. In countries that still have large agricultural populations, these structural changes call for appropriate action in the interests of agriculture itself and of the recipient sectors. In France, where about 14 per cent of the working population are still in agriculture despite the large numbers that have already left the land, the "Fonds d'action sociale pour l'amélioration des structures agricoles"(2) assists farm workers in acquiring training to suit them for other jobs.

In Germany, the Federal Employment Bureau, in co-operation with other appropriate bodies, is making efforts to establish and equip training centres for the working population in rural areas. These centres have to be sited near rural areas so as to be easily accessible, particularly in winter.

A feature of industry during the period covered by the report has been its need for increasingly skilled manpower and, more basically, for manpower capable of adapting to changing needs. Not only has the teaching given during the period of compulsory education had to be adjusted in the light of this fact but also employees have had to be given opportunities to supplement this training or to acquire new skills more relevant to their work. The principle of "continuing education" has already been discussed in many countries.

In Germany, for example, the Federal government action programme for 1970 states: "Basic socio-economic knowledge should be imparted as a universal teaching principle in all classes of schools giving a general education. All pupils in the last three classes should be given instruction in choosing a career, industrial practice and economics. They should be made familiar with various jobs, job categories and their inter-relationships by visiting factories, etc. and doing practical courses in them".

In France, courses in economics and business management have been introduced into standard secondary schools, and university institutes of technology have been set up with the same object in view.

---

1) The Nuremberg Federal Employment Bureau, with its various subordinate bodies, is the principal organisation involved in the regulation of the labour market in Germany. It is very largely self-governing.

2) Social action fund for improving agricultural structures.

TABLE 30

GERMANY

Summary of receipts and expenditure of the

Federal Employment Bureau

(in millions of DM)

	1972	1973	1974	1975
Income	5.767,4	7.469,0	7.985,8	9.233,9
of which contributions	5.077,7	5.828,6	6.443,9	7.786.5
Expenditure				
1. Personal training assistance	1.770,5	1.771,8	2.057,0	2.801,8
initial training	281,0	237,9	210,6	277,4
further training	298,1	233,5	265,3	373,9
retraining	81,0	67,3	87,0	158,8
subsistence allowances during further training and retraining	1.110,4	1.233,2	1.494,2	1.991,4
2. Assistance to training institutions	40,3	48,4	71,0	63,6
3. Assisting entry into employment	113,8	142,5	122,6	186,3
4. Industrial and vocational rehabilitation of handicapped persons	198,6	314,6	393,2	433,7
5. Short-time working allowances	278,8	74,0	677,5	2.207,1
6. Bad weather pay	625,6	510,6	532,3	395,6
7. Aid to increase production of building industry in winter	14,9	47,9	64,9	50,2
8. Other aid payments to building firms and workers	74,7	84,3	22,4	17,2
9. Measures for creating employment	17,1	20,0	32,4	126,7
10. Unemployment benefits	1.283,8	1.394,7	3.551,6	7.765,5
11. Supplementary unemployment benefits	84,4	108,1	222,4	776,2
12. Administrative costs, etc.	1.292,1	1.512,5	1.744,7	2.093,1
Total expenditure	5.794,6	6.807,1	10.352,5	17.835,9
Balance	− 27,2	+ 661,9	− 2.366,7	− 8.602,2

In relation to continuing education, the <u>Australian</u> Government established in 1974 the National Employment and Training System (NEAT). This system is designed to go further than previous employment training programmes, and ultimately to retrain one per cent of the work force every year.

In <u>France</u>, the Act of 18th December, 1963, establishing the Fonds National de l'Emploi, was intended to facilitate the continued activity of workers in dependent employment affected by changes due to economic growth by encouraging their adaptation to new jobs.

In the same field, the Act of 1963 was followed by the Guideline and Programme Act on Vocational Training of 3rd December, 1966 and the Act of 31st December, 1968 on the remuneration of trainees in vocational training courses.

Following an important national inter-trade agreement signed on 9th July, 1970, whereby workers dismissed for economic reasons were guaranteed an income provided they received appropriate vocational training, these Acts were rescinded and replaced by the Act of 16th July, 1971 which established continuing vocational training as part of recurrent education.

Under <u>the national inter-trade agreement of 9th July, 1970</u>, workers who are the victims of a collective dismissal (or an individual dismissal owing to mergers, takeovers or reorganisation - in the case of managerial staff) have the opportunity to follow approved vocational training courses, while continuing to receive all their previous gross pay. The maximum duration of these courses is one year, but no minimum duration is required.

<u>The Act of 1971 on vocational training</u> stipulates that vocational training and social mobility schemes should be the subject of training agreements between the various bodies concerned, i.e. the Government, enterprises, public establishments and workers.

The first practical application of this legislation concerns leave for training: all enterprises which have signed a training agreement are obliged to grant training leave to all workers who request it, provided that the number of hours of leave asked for does not exceed 2 per cent of the total number of hours worked during the year, in the case of establishments employing less than 100 people. In the case of enterprises with 100 employees or more, the number of workers on leave for training purposes cannot exceed 2 per cent of the establishment's total labour force. Leave is the same as the length of the course, i.e. a maximum of one year for full-time courses, or 1,200 hours for those demanding part-time attendance. These limits can, however, be exceeded in the case of so-called "occupational advancement" courses.

The Government gives financial assistance for each of the following types of training:

- "conversion" courses and "prevention" courses: these are
  open to people aged at least 18 who have been dismissed or
  whose jobs are threatened, and who therefore have to envisage
  a change of activity;
- "adaptation" courses: these are intended for holders of work
  contracts who are paid by their enterprise; the object is to
  facilitate access to their new jobs;
- "occupational advancement" courses: these are for workers
  who wish to acquire better qualifications;
- "refresher or further training" courses: the purpose of
  these courses is to maintain the level of skill of workers
  already in employment;
- pre-training and training courses, and preparatory courses
  for working life: these are open to young people aged between
  16 and 18 who do not have work contracts.

In addition, employers help to finance vocational training. In
1972, they had to contribute at least 0.8 per cent of the total
wages paid during the course of the year, and this percentage has increased constantly since. Employers are able to meet this obligation
in several ways.

Under the heading of legislation on vocational training for job
applicants, the Ministry of Labour assumes responsibility for the
conversion and further training of job applicants through the medium
of the Association pour la Formation Professionnelle des Adultes
(AFPA), whose activities it subsidises entirely. The training
schemes provided by the AFPA fall into three main categories: so-
called "traditional" schemes (conversion and prevention), pre-training
schemes for young people leaving school with no qualifications, and
priority schemes under the direct responsibility of the Fonds
National de l'Emploi. The last-mentioned are the result of agreements concluded, in the main, with enterprises with the object of
solving isolated employment problems of a temporary and urgent nature.
The Act of 1971 on vocational training also includes measures specific to young workers or job applicants, as well as to women who
stopped working for a long period in order to raise their children.

Active manpower policy has been intensified as the economic
situation has worsened. The public authorities have mainly insisted
on encouraging vocational training for the unemployed and on the
promotion of employment; recent measures have been aimed at releasing jobs on the labour market.

Vocational training and retraining may be conducted in special
establishments, apprentice schools or technical training centres,
or take the form of on-the-job training.

In certain cases, workers and management may - with government
consent and assistance - jointly seek solutions to the problem of

ensuring that there is continuous effort to match manpower supply to demand. Under the 1965 <u>Canada</u> Manpower Adjustment Programme, for example, the Canadian Government is doing its utmost to persuade workers' and employers' representatives to resolve the manpower problems generated by economic and technological changes which may affect a firm, an industry or a whole region. Financial incentives are available to labour and management to encourage the development of private manpower adjustment programmes through joint consultations and advanced planning, including the assumption by the federal government of up to 50 per cent of the costs involved. In cases where transfer of workers from one facility of a company to another in the same company is part of a private adjustment plan, the federal government may authorize payment of 50 per cent of the cost of such transfers. The next table summarises the measures taken from the implementation of the programme up to 1972 (see Table 20).

1. <u>Vocational training in special establishments</u>

In <u>Great Britain</u> vocational training centres have a very long history, the first having been set up in 1917 to train disabled ex-servicemen. Although the objectives have changed, the role of these centres remains virtually the same and has even been extended. The range of courses offered, originally restricted to manual craft trades, now covers commercial and clerical subjects, semi-skilled industrial trades, technical and professional training as well.

Two categories of worker attend these centres: those who satisfy the entry requirements under the Training Opportunities Scheme (TOPS)(1) and Other Training Arrangements (OTA), operating since 1972, and those sent by their employer under the Sponsored Training Scheme. The Sponsored Training Scheme enables employers to send workers to Skillcentres for intensive training in skilled manual trades which they cannot, for lack of facilities or skilled personnel, provide themselves.

The former category are paid a weekly allowance according to the number of their dependents and a supplement related to their former

---

1) TOPS conditions are that the applicant:

   a) is aged 19 or over and has not been in full-time education for at least three years (exceptions are made for young people who are disabled and for redundant apprentices);
   b) intends to take up new employment in the trade for which he is training;
   c) is prepared to leave his present job to take a training course;
   d) has not had a training course under TOPS or under the Vocational Training Scheme during the previous five years (exceptions may be made for disabled or unemployed people, or for people seeking upgrading training in their training trade;
   e) is suited to his course, suitability being assessed by the Department of Employment.

TABLE 11

CANADA

CANADA MANPOWER ADJUSTMENT PROGRAMME

	Assessment agreements					Mobility agreements				
	Number of assessment agreements	Total cost ($'000)	Federal contribution ($'000)	Number of workers affected	Cost per worker ($)	Number	Total cost ($'00)	Federal contribution ($'000)	Number of workers moved	Cost per worker ($)
Completed programmes	280	1273.0*	591.6	121.675	10.5	105	782.9*	384.2	938	
Programmes in progress	121	1277.3	557.7	128.506	9.9	52	-	50% of the cost		

* Amount subject to change.

earnings. These allowances are worked out to be some £8.30 above
unemployment benefit in order to encourage unemployed persons to
enter training and thus find a new job more easily.

Sponsored training was introduced in 1968 at a time when an increase in the provision for the Government's Training Centres allowed
some training places to be set aside for this purpose. The scheme
was started in response to some demand from employers. The purpose
of the scheme is to use available facilities in training centres to
allow employers who are not adequately equipped, due to lack of
facilities or skilled personnel, to increase their skilled manpower
force by training their existing employees. Sponsored trainees can
be given upgrading training, from unskilled or semi-skilled to skilled
work or from one level of skill to a higher level; conversion training from an existing skill to a new one; or training in dual skills
as may be required to facilitate productivity agreements. Employers
are required to give an undertaking that workers accepted for training will remain in their employment during training, and that the
employer will accept responsibility for their wages, social insurance,
other payments connected with their employment and all other claims
arising from their attendance at a Skillcentre. Sponsored training
is free to employers in Assisted Areas, but charges have been introduced for employers in other areas.

Table 12 shows the increase in the number of trainees in both
categories.

Table 12

GREAT BRITAIN

VOCATIONAL TRAINING: NUMBER OF TRAINEES

Year	TOPS	Sponsored training	Total
1969	13,490	587	14,077
1970	13,605	3,043	16,648
1971	15,527	3,816	19,343
1972	29,019	4,092	33,111
1973	39,930	4,451	44,381
1974	45,500	4,243	49,743
1975	60,700	3,869	64,569

It was envisaged that 80,000 trainees would take advantage of the
Training Opportunities Scheme in 1976 and that a ceiling of 100,000
a year would be reached as soon as possible thereafter.

The Canada Manpower Training Programme, undertaken jointly by
Federal and local authorities reflects this country's special needs.
As well as following courses in basic education or undergoing further
training or retraining, adults may also have to become practised in
the other official languages of the country, knowledge of both being
essential for certain jobs.

In 1972, with a view to increasing the number of people receiving basic training or retraining, the eligibility criteria were relaxed and any adult who had been out of school for at least one year became eligible for further training. To increase the numbers of young people and females attending the centres, an allowance of $30 is payable to adults whose parents (or spouses) are in employment.

The results of this programme are given in Table 14 classified under the various forms of training given by the centres.

The German constitution makes the Länder responsible for all in-school vocational training. However, as explicitly stated in the 1969 Act on Vocational Training and the Employment Promotion Act, further training and retraining are a Federal responsibility. Under the 1971 Employment Act both individuals and training institutes and organisations are eligible for assistance.

Maintenance grants to individuals are paid by the Federal Employment Bureau which also bears all or part of the cost of tuition, teaching supplies, travel, working clothes, accident and sickness insurance and also pays lodging and subsistence allowances where trainees are away from home. The amount of the maintenance grant is indexed. Where candidates do not meet the eligibility criteria, loans for an equivalent amount may be granted to cover the maintenance allowance and other expenses.

Table 13

GERMANY

PROMOTION OF VOCATIONAL TRAINING AND RETRAINING

UNDER THE EMPLOYMENT PROMOTION ACT

Year	Expenditure (in millions of DM)	Number of participants
- Promotion of vocational training and retraining (including subsidies) for vocational adjustment)		
1971	1,215	288,390
1972	1,490	260,285
1973	1,534	226,942
1974	1,846	232,597
1975	2,524	270,853
- Promotion of training		
1971	324	249,078
1972	345	265,707
1973	352	241,143
1974	376	199,550
1975	511	not yet known
- Institutional promotion of vocational training		
1971	29.8	
1972	40.3	
1973	48.4	
1974	71.0	
1975	63.6	

TABLE 14

CANADA MANPOWER TRAINING PROGRAMME

NUMBER OF CLIENTS

	Skill	Language	Basic Training for skilled development	Apprentices	Training in industry (1)	Total	Total Expenditure	Cost per client($)
1970-71	155,719	13,193	97,136	53,923	24,875	344,846	289,576,786	839,7
1971-72	143,828	12,527	74,124	46,153	31,520	308,152	328,436,711	1065,8
1972-73	163,674	10,940	60,718	40,369	40,487	316,188	343,497,519	1086,4

Incentives are given to training establishments in the form of grants or loans for the purpose of organising, developing and equipping centres for training, further training and retraining. In special cases (e.g. training establishments for handicapped persons) this assistance may be extended to cover day-to-day running costs. If necessary, the Federal Bureau is empowered to set up its own centres.

2. Training in industry

This is the traditional form of training and adds the practical aspect which formal instruction does not always provide; thus in Germany, under the "double training" system the young person on leaving school may divide his time between apprenticeship in the works and attending courses in a trade school one day per week.

Apart from this aspect of training in industry, many employers now realise the wisdom of developing the skills of their employees to keep pace with technological change. They sometimes receive government assistance for this purpose as part of public policy for matching manpower supply to demand.

In Canada, "Training in Industry" was originally a component of the Canada Manpower Training Programme. The ministry grants employers up to 75 per cent of the cost of training their employees.

It was decided in 1971 to take Training in Industry out of the general programme and incorporate it in the new Canada Manpower Industrial Training Programme which will also include the Canada Manpower Training On-the-Job Programme.

The objectives of the Canada Manpower Industrial Training Programme are "to encourage and assist employers to engage a substantial number of unemployed, unskilled and disadvantaged persons to teach them on-the-job skills that are transferable between employers which will increase their employability or earning capacity and prepare them to take advantage of future employment growth". To this end employers receive grants covering part of trainees' wages during the training period.

Table 15

CANADA

FIGURES RELATING TO THE MANPOWER TRAINING ON-THE-JOB PROGRAMME

Year	Number of trainees	Total cost ($ ' 000)	Cost per trainee
1971-72	43,948	50,922	$1,169
1972-73	36,643	60,594	$1,654

In Great Britain, under the powers conferred by the Employment and Training Act 1973, the Training Services Agency of the Manpower Services Commission provides a number of services to firms who want assistance with the training of their own employees. The services are as follows:

i) Firms may send their employees to be trained as instructors at special training units. This service began in 1962 and was originally provided by the Department of Employment.

ii) The Agency may lend its own instructors to train workers in intermediate skills in engineering or allied trades in a firm's own workshops.
The instructors will also assist the firm's nominees to take over training from them. This "Mobile Instructor" service has operated since 1966, again originally provided by the Department of Employment.

iii) The Agency provides a comprehensive supervisory training service in industry and commerce. Courses are presented which are designed to improve the efficiency of first and second line supervisors covering job instruction and communication, job methods, job relations and job safety.
Ad-hoc courses may be presented to meet the particular needs of an organisation for training supervisory grades. Firms' own training officers may be trained to present these courses. This service dates back to 1945 and was previously the responsibility of the Department of Employment.

"Training within Industry" courses were introduced as a wartime measure to train supervisors in more efficient instructional techniques. The "Mobile Instructor" service was conceived as an auxiliary regional inducement to firms in Development Areas by helping them increase their stock of skilled labour. Training in Instructor Training Colleges was first made available in response to demand from industry and to help industry increase its own training provision.

All these services are free in the Assisted Areas. Elsewhere an economic fee is charged.

Table 25 illustrates the activities of the Training Services Agency and its predecessors in direct training assistance.

Apart from the activities of the Agency, grants have been available since 1965, under the 1964 Industrial Training Act, covering 25 per cent of approved current expenses(1) for five years for each additional training place. Grants are paid to employers through

_____

1) Approved expenses include: Travelling expenses; subsistence allowance; instructor's wages and related costs; general water rates plus costs; charges for heat, light, power and cleaning; cost of materials used for training.

Table 16

GREAT BRITAIN

DIRECT TRAINING ASSISTANCE PROVIDED
BY THE TRAINING SERVICES AGENCY

Year	Number of instructors trained in Instructor Training Colleges or Units	Number of workers trained by the Mobile Instructor Service	Income from Training within Industry courses
1968/69	2,802	196	£287,818
1969/70	3,684	247	314,347
1970/71	3,409	516	354,965
1971/72	2,832	473	325,176
1972/73	3,580	684	322,920
1973/74	3,679	915	361,722
1974/75	3,946	1,196	449,836

Industrial Training Boards and are thus available only to those industries for which there is an Industrial Training Board. The purpose of the grant is to secure a permanent increase in off-the-job training facilities. Since this grant was introduced in 1965 there have been two new schemes introduced.

a) A special loan sanction programme for extra training places in colleges;

b) Economic fees for industrial training provided in colleges.

The introduction of these led to the decision to phase out this scheme.

Funds expended from financial year 1967/68 to financial year 1973/74 totalled £14,882,985. For the period 1st January 1973 to 31st March 1974 the number of additional training places for which grants were paid was 34,532.

B. GEOGRAPHICAL MOBILITY

1. Internal migration

Whereas regional policy is designed to move firms generating employment into areas where manpower is available, policies framed to increase the geographical mobility of manpower do the reverse. In regional development schemes, however, these two types of policy are complementary, not in conflict.

Generally, there are two obstacles in the way of achieving geographical mobility. Firstly, there is the natural reluctance to pull up one's roots and whilst this psychological difficulty is relatively less of a problem in the United States, it may be serious in other countries, e.g. France. Secondly, there is the lack of available housing in growth areas.

The problem is complex particularly in countries where housing availabilities are relatively limited. Providing housing where it is needed calls for accurate forecasting and vigorous action.

In spite of these two obstacles - and frequently to help over-come them - various measures are taken depending on the circumstances in each case. A worker may make a permanent move and take his family with him when he changes his job or the move may be only temporary, a matter of preparing for a new occupation, say at a training centre or with a company wishing to train him before offering a permanent job. Assistance is necessary to facilitate both types of movements as a means of making occupational mobility a reality.

In Canada, as we have seen, a substantial proportion of dis-bursements under the Canada Manpower Adjustment Programme goes to the promotion of geographical mobility.

Under the Canada Manpower Mobility Programme, a specific scheme for assisting the relocation of labour, the government can make grants to workers seeking employment to cover their transport and living costs and possibly give financial assistance to dependents. Relocation grants and allowances for house-hunting etc. are available for those who find suitable employment. The programme is also used - and this seems its commonest application - to aid persons who are enrolled under the Canada Manpower Training Programme in a training centre located outside their area of residence.

Table 17

CANADA

NUMBER OF PERSONS ASSISTED UNDER
THE CANADA MANPOWER MOBILITY PROGRAMME

Year	Number of per-sons assisted in seeking em-ployment	Number of per-sons relocated	Number of trainees	Total cost (dollars)
1970-71	7,370	6,382	71,094	7,285,905
1971-72	7,774	9,026	54,079	8,897,072
1972-73	10,725	10,653	50,296	11,599,984

In Germany, the services provided by the Federal Employment Bureau include meeting the costs of recruitment, travel, relocation and tools, and the grant of bridging loans and resettlement allowances.

The results of this programme are given in Table 18.

Table 18

GERMANY

Year	Expenditure by the Board (DM million)	Number of recipients
1971	60.5	241,390
1972	44.4	198,766
1973	52.4	216,603
1974	67.4	292,864
1975	154.0	404,389

The Bureau has made a special effort to encourage people to take up employment in Berlin. In 1975 it spent DM.19.4 million in 9,845 cases.

The "Programme to promote Employment and Growth in Conditions of Stability", adopted by the Federal Government in December 1974, provides inter alia for a non-recurring mobility grant to be paid to workers unemployed for an extended period of time in order to make it easier for them to accept employment elsewhere. This grant varies between DM.300 and a maximum of DM.600 for each month of unemployment provided the new job is taken prior to May 1.

In Great Britain, an employment transfer scheme has existed, in one form or another, since the war. Today it complements the Government's regional policies.

Since April 1972, workers whose homes before transfer were in assisted areas receive additional financial assistance under the Employment Transfer Scheme.

Since 1951, key workers who are transferred to help set up or extend a works in a assisted area can claim allowances under the Key Workers Scheme.

In both these cases, assistance consists of grants for allowances in respect of fares, lodging costs and household removal expenses and may be given for up to two years from the date of transfer.

The Nucleus Labour Force Scheme was introduced in 1946. It provides for the payment of fares and lodging allowances to unemployed workers who are recruited in areas of high unemployment by employers who are setting up or extending establishments in those areas and who transfer the workers to parent factories for training. On completion of this training the workers return to their home areas for employment in the new or extended factories. In all cases the transfers are temporary and assistance is normally given for up to 6 months.

Table 19 shows the number of workers assisted under the three schemes, together with the total cost.

Table 19

GREAT BRITAIN

Year	Number of workers assisted			Cost £ 000
	Employment Transfer Scheme	Key Worker Scheme	Nucleus Labour Force Scheme	
1975–76	15 701	435	7	5 965
1974–75	14 333	753	34	4 372
1973–74	15 237	691	67	4 600
1972–73	18 557	792	57	4 433
1971–72	8 405	739	79	1 600
1970–71	7 200	801	57	890
1969–70	6 344	512	402	663
1968–69	6 091	369	261	581

In addition, on 5th November, 1975 the Job Search Scheme was introduced which assisted workers with fares for job interviews beyond daily travelling distance of their homes, and paid lodging costs to allow workers to spend periods of time away from their homes to look for work.

In Spain the existing boundaries of the major industrial development zone in Galicia have been modified in 1975.

By extending the geographical limits in order to take best advantage of the great industrial development zone of Galicia, this measure aims at reducing migration from this area towards other more industrialised regions of Spain or to foreign countries.

2. External migration

In certain countries, such as Australia, the only way to meet certain manpower requirements is to bring in foreign workers. Policies designed to facilitate geographic mobility are thus supplemented by an immigration policy which is generally selective, admitting only those workers able to contribute to economic growth.

In Germany, the high growth rate during the sixties attracted large numbers of foreign workers. Their number rose from 167,000 in 1959 to 2,595,000 in September, 1975, when they accounted for 11.9 per cent of the Federal Republic's workforce. In September 1975, 2,038,000 foreign workers were employed in the Federal Republic of Germany.

Foreign manpower is more mobile than indigenous labour, but a considerable effort is required on the part of central and local authorities, and philanthropic organisations to assist foreign workers.

The Federal Labour Board has made loans from its resources to finance the construction of 2,925 residences for 187,000 immigrant workers, spending about DM.465 million for this purpose up to 1975. In addition an amount of 45 million was spent for the promotion of housing (5,150 units) in favour of immigrant workers. The Federal and Länder Governments and the Federal Board also spent more than DM.100 million between 1966 and 1975 on measures designed to give immigrants a better life away from work.

C. GUARANTEED INCOMES

Most systems of guaranteed incomes organised by the public authorities or arranged by agreement between employers and employees were brought in to offset the effects of cyclical fluctuations in economic activity. However, there is increasing awareness of their value in relation to the structural changes inherent in economic growth.

In spite of the efforts made by the public authorities to facilitate industrial adjustment, the complexity and rigidity of the production system are such that there are bound to be times when employees are thrown out of work or reduced to short-time working. A symptom of the changes taking place in the structure of the economy, loss of employment is generally a consequence of firms closing down. However, being out of a job is sometimes unavoidable in order to train in other skills or to learn another job. Measures encouraging manpower mobility, therefore, have to be backed up by guaranteed income schemes.

The form of assistance depends on the particular situation. Unemployment may be total or only a matter of short-time working, it may be limited to certain periods or affect more particularly certain types of employee. Sometimes it is only in prospect. The authorities may help to lighten the burden on the enterprise or even assist it to weather a particularly difficult period.

In France, for example, it is common for a firm with liquidity problems to be allowed to defer payment of its social security contributions; however, all too often bankruptcy cannot be avoided and the social security system is unable to collect the debt in full.

In Sweden, apart from the large number of legislative provisions concerning the employment market, grants have been available since 1972, to firms in temporary difficulties. Only firms employing

more than 50 people are eligible. The grant is paid for a maximum
of six months and its amount cannot normally exceed one-third of the
total wage bill. There has been very limited use of this facility.

In _Australia_, guaranteed incomes under the structural adjustment
assistance program are made available direct to the worker. An employee who is unemployed as a direct result of structural change for
which the Government has prescribed adjustment assistance, is entitled to income maintenance equal to his average weekly earnings
(less overtime) for the previous six months, for a period of six
months. This system was introduced in 1973 as part of the (then)
interim adjustment program.

In certain countries benefits are provided not only for total
loss of employment but also to compensate for a loss in earnings due
to short-time working.

In _Italy_, blue and white-collar workers in industry are paid an
allowance from the Unemployment Fund for an indefinite period if
they lose their jobs or are put on short-time because of sectoral or
local economic difficulties or because the firm employing them is
being restructured or reorganised. These allowances amount to about
80 per cent of gross pay in all cases with a ceiling of L.200,000
for white-collar workers. The government's contribution to the
Unemployment Fund is L.20,000 million a year, the remainder of its
resources coming from employers.

In _Germany_, the Federal Employment Board pays unemployment and
short-time working benefits.

As of 1st January 1975 unemployment benefit comes to 68 per
cent of wages reduced by statutory deductions to which employees are
normally subject. In addition to that, unemployed persons may receive child allowances under a new system.

In the case of extraordinary conditions on the labour market the
Federal Minister for Labour and Social Affairs may provide by decree
that the period set for receiving short-time benefit

- shall be extended up to 12 months in the case of extraordinary
  conditions in specific industrial branches or districts,
- shall be extended up to 24 months in the case of extraordinary
  conditions on the labour market as a whole. As of the time
  of writing, the maximum period is thus 24 months.

Benefits for loss of earnings may sometimes be payable when
work is interrupted by weather conditions, generally in the construction industry. In _Germany_, these allowances have accounted for nearly
one-third of the total disbursements of the Federal Employment Board.
A number of measures were introduced in 1972 designed to reduce this
expenditure by encouraging employers to provide work throughout the
year. Both employees and employers in the construction industry are
affected by the measures.

Employees are paid:

- a "winter allowance" of DM2 from the Federal Board for every
  hour worked in the winter season covered by the assistance
  procedure;
- bad weather benefits for every hour of work lost during the
  winter season.

Employers receive:

- grants or loans equivalent to 50 per cent of money spent on
  aids designed to allow work to continue during the winter;
- extra-expense grants to meet the higher costs involved in
  winter working.

An allowance is sometimes paid to make up for a drop in earnings
as a result of changing jobs. Miners, for example, who receive substantial fringe benefits, stand to lose these if they switch to other
jobs where their skills are no longer required. Under the redeploy-
ment scheme introduced in the European Community countries, miners
are paid an allowance as an incentive to take less well-paid jobs.
Under this E.C.S.C. system miners receive a change-of-job allowance
and are guaranteed between 90 and 100 per cent of their previous
earnings for a period of one year.

In connection with the already mentioned "Programme to promote
Employment and Growth in Conditions of Stability" adopted in
December 1974, and with a view to reducing unemployment, a wage cost
subsidy will be paid to employers recruiting unemployed labour for
other than temporary employment prior to May 1, 1975, thus extending
their staff. The wage cost subsidy will be equal to 60 per cent of
the gross wages over a period of six months. The subsidy will be
paid in a lump sum upon recruitment of the unemployed worker.

SUMMARY AND CONCLUSIONS BASED ON
PARTS I AND II OF THE REPORT

Over and above differences in the motivation behind and mechanisms of the fiscal and financial industrial policy instruments
enumerated and analysed in Parts I and II of the report, there are
many similarities between one group of instruments and another as
regards the principles which govern them. Such differences as there
are, moreover, can be largely attributed to economic and industrial
situations and trends peculiar to each country. The main object in
fact is to allow or to facilitate the transfer of resources to industry in pursuance of the specific development or adaptation objectives of the public authorities' policy. Since these transfers are
effected on terms which are favourable in relation mainly to a given
situation (in the case of fiscal instruments) or to existing market
conditions, for comparable risks and guarantees, (in the case of financial instruments), their impact can be assessed according to the
capacity of the incentive to influence the entrepreneur's behaviour.
This behaviour is itself, however, part of an economic and industrial
context and development outlook which together determine the alternative choices and decisions open to the entrepreneur and the impact
of the advantage obtained.

To go back to the aims of the report as originally stated, it
is reasonable by way of conclusion to consider what lessons it contains regarding the degree of generalisation and the nature of the
instruments in question, the volume of resources transferred and
their impact and effectiveness in relation to the objectives they
are set.

Given the approach adopted for the purposes of this report, i.e.
the establishment of a relationship between fiscal and financial instruments and a certain number of objectives peculiar to industrial
policy, it was possible to draw up, in more systemized form, a matrix
of the various fiscal and financial instruments in use in the countries which replied to the questionnaire. Because of the relative
diversity of the techniques and methods used and objectives pursued,
this systemization was valuable. Owing to the fact that it can be
inflexible, this presentation had to be supplemented by an analysis
of the particularities of each type of instrument, taking account

131

as far as the available information allowed of the circumstances accompanying both their introduction and their continued use. This is because a brief description of an objective can in many cases have a different meaning according to whether the context in which it is placed is essentially cyclical or structural, horizontal or vertical, for example. Likewise, objectives sometimes change in nature depending, in particular, on the trend in the situation or industrial problems.

It also emerges from the report that the number of instruments at present used in all the countries considered together was growing markedly during the past decade up until the period covered by the report. This increase can be ascribed to mainly a threefold phenomenon.

In the first place, there has been a substantial increase in collective responsibilities on the part of the public authorities. In many countries, this has resulted in a marked rise in public expenditure which has had a twofold effect on industry: a relative reduction in the resources available for its development, i.e. in the remuneration of factors of production, and also an increase in the charges that enterprises must pay in order to finance this expenditure.

Secondly, the fact that an increasingly effective battery of instruments had to be developed in response to the growing variety of problems, or their perception, with which industry is faced, is due in part to the greater pressures and constraints it is facing in areas such as protection of the consumer and of the environment. It is also due, moreover, to the need to approach problems in global terms - in particular by gradually incorporating in industrial policy considerations relating specifically for example to technology and manpower - and therefore frame instruments capable of assisting enterprises to solve every aspect of the problems or situations encountered with the consequences this can have regarding the consistency of the way in which instruments are used.

Lastly, the degree of diversification of industrial policy instruments can be explained in many cases by the different stages of development reached by the various countries, and the realisation that these call for specific solutions. The requirements and problems of an industry in an economy moving towards the primacy of the service sector differ considerably from those of an industry which is part of an agricultural and craft economy. While in the first case it is frequently a question of adjusting production structures which are often of long-standing to meet the pressures and constraints of trends in demand, in the second case it is mainly a question of creating and developing production structures - it being clear that none of the countries considered has an economy which can be neatly inserted in one or other of the categories envisaged.

While the means of carrying out transfers have, apparently, increased in number and become more varied in response to the growing variety of problems, it is also important to consider the overall volume of resources transferred, either directly or indirectly. The information available concerning the volume of financial resources allocated to or used by different instruments has been systemized and grouped by country and by main instrument. However, the level and trend of the overall volume are still difficult to determine. This is doubtless due in the first place to the inherent difficulties of apprehending flows, distinguishing them from other economic flows and/or flows depending on other policies, and comparing, in particular, flows resulting from fiscal with those from financial instruments.

Secondly, the information available often relates to a fairly limited number of years during which the influence of fluctuations caused by cyclical factors could have been significant and perhaps difficult to eliminate. Lastly, an examination of the volume of funds would have to be directed towards the problem of deflating sums in money terms, i.e. it would have to contemplate creating a specific deflator in order to be able to eliminate purely monetary fluctuations. In some cases, such as instruments for promoting investment for example, any increase in money terms would also have to be examined in the light of the parallel trend in ratios such as the capital/output ratio, in order to be better able to evaluate its development.

The impact of industrial policy instruments, in accordance with the objectives of this policy as regards the quest for efficiency, should be capable of evaluation from the point of view of their impact on the productivity level of the recipient enterprise or enterprises and, via them, on other industrial enterprises, by means of market mechanisms. Any incentive transfer of resources to an enterprise should in time produce an additional surplus inside this enterprise, either by developing its known activities (increasing production capacity for example), or by means of changes in its production apparatus (modernisation of means of production, rationalisation of product lines or partial or total conversion to other activities).

Knowledge of the effect of industrial policy instruments is therefore closely bound up in the first place with the use by enterprises of the instruments in question. It transpires, however, in many cases that for very different reasons, which can depend in particular on the mechanism of a particular instrument, the impact can focus on certain categories of enterprise, depending on their size, location, traditions and knowledge of the public authorities' methods of action, for example, without this pattern of impact necessarily corresponding to the optimum use of the instruments.

To the extent that an industrial policy is necessarily based on action taken and results achieved in the past, on which it may be necessary to act on to allow for new considerations, knowledge of the real impact of existing instruments is essential in order to be able to distinguish clearly the possible options, bearing in mind the overall allocation of available resources.

Lastly, knowledge of flows can be assessed in the light of the very variable capacity of enterprises to attain the degree of economic efficiency required by the necessity to be or to become competitive, in other words to produce the surplus productivity sought after in applying industrial policy instruments. This capacity varies considerably according, in particular, to certain factors which have already been mentioned, and also to the degree of competition on the markets and the enterprises' production structures, for example. If certain flows persist for longer than may be thought necessary for the ordered progress of the development or adaptation process, this may be due to the difficulty of assessing this capacity - it being understood that only objectives specific to industrial policy are considered here.

Over and above determining the immediate impact of industrial policy instruments, it is necessary to consider the volume and nature of the impact which affects, via the recipients, the whole fabric of industry, both domestic and international. The behaviour of each enterprise in the distribution of the surplus thus created becomes of vital importance at this stage: relative trend of prices and improvement of related services and trend in the respective remuneration of factors of production, for example. It is at this level that it is possible to evaluate two distinct phenomena, which are nevertheless very closely linked by virtue of their potential impact on the allocation of resources at national or international level. The first phenomenon concerns transfers of resources between sectors by means of the price mechanism. An enterprise or sector which is receiving government assistance can be induced to keep price levels below those needed in order to ensure that its factors of production are adequately remunerated, and thereby contribute to transfers of resources to other branches of industry for example, and vice versa, depending in particular on the level of competition on the market. The second phenomenon concerns international competition and the effect that the assisted creation of additional productivity passed on in the direct or indirect components of the price structure can have on the allocation of international resources.

The objectives of the report included, lastly, an analysis of the effectiveness of the instruments considered in the report, i.e. the aim was to compare the amount of the incentive element contained in each instrument with the volume of resources transferred in the

context of the objectives originally fixed. Apart from the pre-
liminary difficulties, as it were, which have already been mentioned
above, an exercise of this type comes up against a number of difficulties of some consequence. In the first place, with regard to defining the objective or objectives to be taken into consideration,
it was very clear from the information available that to determine
a specific objective cannot be considered a realistic approach. It
transpires in fact most of the time that several objectives overlap
without there being any precise order of priority, or else they can
change over time. Secondly, as far as the instruments are concerned,
and as has already been emphasised several times in the report, the
rule seems to be to use a combination of different instruments in
order to solve problems which have a number of different aspects.
It would therefore seem advisable to use the notion of a plan or
project in considering this question. Finally, as has just been
stressed with regard to the subject of impact, there is as yet little
information in the report on the behaviour of enterprises and the
factors which have a decisive influence on their decision-making
processes. Last of all, the criteria used for assessment are too
numerous to be reduced to a review of industrial effectiveness.
Like industrial policy itself, its instruments are obviously part of
a vaster economic framework, and their effectiveness could perhaps
be assessed mainly in the light of their contribution to the accom-
plishment of overall economic policy objectives.

Part III

THE SPECIAL CASE OF
SMALL AND MEDIUM-SIZED FIRMS

INTRODUCTORY SURVEY

A. THE PROBLEM OF DEFINITIONS

The formulation of policies addressed to a given category of
enterprises, for example in relation to their sectoral identity or
their size group, calls for a more or less explicit definition of
the sub-category involved. It is clear that size groups - wherever
one places the line of demarcation - comprise a continuity, and even
a slight displacement of such a boundary line could lead to the in-
clusion, or exclusion, of a significant number of potential benefi-
ciaries with respect to whatever aids or facilities may be provided
for the group in question. The process of definition is thus a
matter of importance; and the difficulty noted above is perhaps not
unrelated to the fact that in certain countries, few or no measures,
apart perhaps from certain tax provisions, have been addressed exclusively to Small and Medium-sized Businesses (SMB's).

Once the process of definition is initiated, it is important,
first of all, to keep in mind that the concept of size, whatever measure is used in applying it, is of necessity a relative notion and
must be considered in the context of the size of the economy concerned and the degree of industrial concentration. It is necessary
also to determine the statistical unit to be measured, since an
enterprise involves economic realities (e.g., a unit or units of
production) as well as legal realities (a company or other legally
designated entity).

One criterion frequently resorted to is the number of persons
employed. The practice of using this criterion may result more from
certain statistical limitations - since the number of persons employed is the most generally available datum - than from thorough
analysis. Exclusive reference to persons employed leaves out of
consideration numerous other, and economically significant, ways of
looking at "size" (and the resort to employment figures may also
encounter complications resulting from the prevalence of seasonal
fluctuations in certain industries). A number of governments have,
in fact, either in general definitions or in relation to specific
legislative programmes, not used the employment criterion or supplemented it with parameters expressed in monetary terms e.g., the

value of assets or turnover. In Japan, for example, the legislation on the promotion of SMB's covers enterprises employing fewer than 300 persons or having a registered capital of less than 100 million yen. It should be noted that the reference to a criterion involving a monetary measure implies a need to take periodic account of inflation in order to readjust the ceilings that have been set.

The definition of SMB used may also need to be adapted to the nature and objectives of the relevant policy measure. For example, in the case of tax measures, it may be advisable for eligibility to be determined, at least in part, in accordance with the particular type of tax involved (e.g., tax on profits, added value tax) and with the level of taxes that would have been payable in the absence of specific measures in favour of the SMB's.

Finally, the sub-category of firms considered under the label SMB is far from being homogeneous. It would seem desirable for certain purposes to recognise the specificity of, e.g., highly technology-oriented firms dependent upon risk capital, those heavily engaged in manufacture on a sub-contracting basis, etc., and to shape policies in accordance with such diversity.

Apart from the quantitative approaches noted above, a full typology(1) would also have to refer to other characteristics of a qualitative nature, which, even if they cannot be used in determining eligibility criteria, may be suggestive of possible policy approaches to SMBs. To take just one example: one of the advantages that the smaller firms may have is their flexibility, their capacity to adapt to variations in demand and to exploit new opportunities; and this advantage is not unrelated to the fact that in numerous smaller firms the decision-making power is still in the hands of one or a very small number of persons.

B. THE IMPORTANCE OF SMB's

Before surveying the problems of the SMB's, a brief word about the place they occupy in country economies. We shall refer to size categories of firms as the only readily available definitional criterion for such broad international generalisations. If we consider only those firms having fewer than 50 persons employed, it is seen that in the industrialised countries the number of such firms represents roughly anywhere from about three-quarters to over nine-tenths

---

1) The Commission of the European Communities has in a document
   /413/111/76 f/ assembled the definitions most commonly used in the
   nine Member countries. The foreword to this document notes that
   there exists no legal definition in these countries of the small
   and medium-sized enterprise (SMB), although there exists such a
   definition for the craft enterprise in Germany, France, Italy and
   Belgium.

of all industrial enterprises. The share of total industrial employment accounted for by such firms is highly variable (only 12 per cent
in Germany but as much as 43 per cent in Japan in 1966, with other
industrialised countries generally falling somewhere in between) as
is their share of total industrial production (only 10 per cent in
Germany but 30 per cent in Norway (1967).

When one considers that in many cases the extremely varied em-
ployment-based definitions of SMB's may include firms having up to
100, 300 or 500 persons employed, the brief sketch of the place oc-
cupied by those with fewer than 50 employees clearly shows the importance to national economies of problems related to SMB's. Moreover,
both the economic and social aspects of these problems must be seen
in the light of the fact that while large numbers of smaller firms
are to be found in very many sectors, they predominate particularly
in such traditional industries as textiles and clothing, leather and
wood-working - which, in turn, are often concentrated in certain
geographical areas, in these cases adding a regional dimension to
to the problems.

C. THE PROBLEMS FACED BY SMB's

Small firms appear to be faced today with three types of problem.
Firstly, they do not always find the support they need for their development in the economic environment in which they are operating;
secondly, their internal structures are often outdated; and thirdly,
the businessmen involved may lack the necessary skills in management
techniques. Government action generally relates to these three
areas: general conditions, internal structure and manpower efficiency.

Measures affecting general conditions are designed to provide
easier access to capital, to help in opening markets up at home and
abroad and to improve access to, and participation in, Government
contracts, to define small firms' situation in relation to the larger
ones and to simplify what is required of them under the legislation
and regulations in force.

Measures relating to firms themselves are designed to raise the
level of technology, in particular by encouraging the introduction
of new production processes or the improvement of existing ones.
Another objective may be to help small firms to join forces in order
to become more competitive.

Lastly, as far as manpower problems are concerned, government
assistance may be aimed at introducing modern management techniques
and increasing the level of skill of employees.

We shall, therefore, in Chapters 7 to 9, deal in turn with policies concerning these three areas. Under each of them, the aims indicated in the questionnaire break down in the following way:

I. Economic, Financial and Legal Conditions

Aims

15. Access to capital.
17. Product marketing:
    - on the home market;
    - on the international market.
22. Access to and participation in government contracts.
23. Position vis-à-vis bigger enterprises.
24. Compliance with administrative or regulatory requirements.

II. The Firms Themselves

Aims

16. Introduction of new processes, techniques or their improvement.
18. Concentration/integration - co-operation/association.
19. Creation of technology-based enterprises.

III. Manpower Problems

Aims

20. Training of management in management techniques.
21. Employment of highly qualified manpower.

Further objectives indicated by the different countries will be dealt with under each of these three main headings.

D. POLICY INSTRUMENTS AND MECHANISMS

Three sorts of instruments - fiscal, financial and service-type - will be referred to.

In most countries, fiscal legislation appears to pay no regard to size of firm. Comments under this heading in parts I and II of this Report therefore apply fully to small and medium-sized businesses and will not be repeated here.

Since service-type instruments are not covered by Questionnaire I, some countries have pointed out that all firms are entitled to use them. In fact, they are mainly used in relation to small and medium-sized businesses since they take the place of certain functions that are already part of the structure of large firms.

Some instruments may have highly specific objectives whereas others may relate to very general areas, making classification diffi-cult under the objectives listed above. In the United Kingdom, for example, the 10 Small Firms Information Centres (the first of which was opened in 1973) have a wide spectrum of objectives. The purposes of these centres are:

a) To provide owners and staff of small businesses with a single regional point of reference that can introduce them to the most appropriate sources of help that are available;

b) To provide a feedback to Government on matters concerning small firms, their worries and how Government and other legislation affects their operation;

c) To maximise the use of Britain's information services by ensuring that small firms are made aware of the facilities available to them covering such things as banking, marketing, technical and administrative problems.

All ten centres planned are now open at a total cost of £350,000. The service is free to small firms.

In most countries government measures have been decided to meet the specific requirements of small firms as each need arose. But today, in certain countries, the experience that has been gained is leading not only to a change in administrative structures, but also to a consolidation of the administrative machinery used.

In Canada, for example, the proposal to set up a Federal Business Development Bank (the Bill for this had been introduced before the dissolution of the House of Commons in May 1974) stemmed from the feeling that the information, advisory, training and financing services previously provided through the various government programmes should be grouped together.

On the other hand, the need to decentralise action by the authorities to achieve closer contact with smaller and medium-sized firms spread across the national territory often means that certain organisations have to be set up between the centres of decision on industrial policy and the points where it is applied. These agencies are operated jointly by Government authorities and the industries concerned, the ratio between the two varying from country to country. In some cases these organisations may play a major role.

In Sweden, for example, aid to small and medium-sized enterprises is mainly handled through the 24 Business Development Associations (B.D.A.) whose objective is to promote craft trades and small-scale industry in their County. They administer most government programmes and they have a very wide range of functions covering all the services now available to small firms: credit, information and advice.

Specialists in these associations give technical and economic advice and information free of charge. Only in-depth studies have to be paid for. This government programme, handled by the National Industry Board, cost Kr.2.5 million in 1973/74 and Kr.4.8 million in 1974/75.

These Associations have a dual function in the distribution of public money. They scrutinise applications and ensure that loans on concessionary terms, a facility available since 1960, are allocated as they should be. They also give advice, case by case, as to whether the Government should give its guarantee for bank loans taken out by small firms. Table 1 summarises their activity.

Table 1

SWEDEN

ACTIVITY OF BUSINESS DEVELOPMENT ASSOCIATIONS

1970-1973

Loans granted in	1970	1971	1972
Amount (Kr. million)	78	75	92
Number	1073	979	1004
Insured loans in	1970/71	1971/72	1972/73
Amount (Kr. million)	32	67	62
Number	57	116	105

At 30th June 1973 the fund totalled Kr.325 million. At 31st December outstanding loans amounted to Kr.272 million. The ceiling for loans is currently Kr.200,000.

The total value of insured loans is Kr.260 million, the average insured loan being Kr.590,000. Guarantees must not exceed a cumulative value of Kr.100 million a year.

With reference to overall policy and administrative mechanisms, there has been a clear tendency over the years to create special foci of responsibility with respect to SMB's. An early manifestation of this was the establishment of the United States Small Business Administration, initially as part of the Department of Commerce and subsequently separated as an independent agency of the Executive Branch.

Much more recently, in France, as from 1969, a Secretary of State, and then a Minister, have had special responsibilities with regard to small and medium-sized firms. In the United Kingdom a Small Firms Division was set up at the Department of Industry in 1971. The report of the (Bolton) Committee of enquiry has shown that the roughly 1,250,000 small firms employed about one-quarter of the working population and were producing about 20 per cent of the G.N.P.

In Australia, the National Small Business Bureau was established in 1974. The Bureau's programme embraces research and policy work

associated with the operation of small business, management development (encompassing training and counselling), collection and dissemination of technological and economic information, and other
appropriate advisory services. However, the most important function
of the Bureau is the co-ordination of existing facilities and services provided by the Government and private sectors. For instance,
in the marketing of exports, the Export Finance and Insurance
Corporation acting as both an export financing facility and an export
insurance agency is available to handle the needs of both small and
large businesses. In the area of finance for small businesses, the
Commonwealth Development Bank has since its inception in 1960 had a
mandate to provide finance for the establishment or development of
industrial undertakings, particularly small undertakings.

Chapter 7

ASSISTANCE WITH REGARD TO THE CONDITIONS IN WHICH
SMALL AND MEDIUM-SIZED ENTERPRISES OPERATE

A. INTRODUCTION

In this field government assistance often was first a matter
of providing SMB's with easier access to capital. Export promotion
policies have also involved governments in helping them to market
their products, particularly in the case of countries where the
number of small firms is large. Apart from bringing in more foreign
currency, larger markets give opportunities for economies of scale.
At the same time, some governments, wishing to provide conditions of
fair and healthy competition with larger firms, have made regulations
defining the relationships between firms of differing size and power.
Another measure taken to ensure that a balance is maintained, is to
give small firms preferential treatment as regards access to, and
participation in, government contracts, the latter sometimes being
organised specifically for them. Lastly, the management of small
firms is sometimes made easier by simplifying the requirements imposed on them by legislation and regulations.

B. ACCESS TO CAPITAL

1. Introduction

This is one of the major problems of small and medium-sized
firms. With their limited financial potential, the usual capital
markets are sometimes not readily available to them. To reduce this
handicap they may join forces and go guarantor for each other,
governments often urging them to take this step. Mutual guarantee
companies of this kind exist in all regions of Italy, for example.
In Japan, too, there are guarantee associations in each prefecture.
A semi-public establishment - the Small and Medium Enterprise Credit
Insurance Corporation - provides the second stage guarantee. The
guaranteed liability balance amounted to Yen 2,378,200 million on
31st March 1974.

145

Apart from the credit facilities that certain governments offer to all firms, special arrangements have been instituted for small and medium-sized firms. The familiar techniques are used: grants, loans on the same terms as those available on the capital market or on concessionary terms, and above all, guarantees, which constitute the most convenient and least costly method for the authorities. This method does not distort competition since its effect is to enable small firms to obtain terms available to larger firms because of their size.

Financial assistance, generally decentralised, is often accompanied by technical and economic support provided by the organisations dispensing the aid.

Easier access to capital may be provided for all small firms or, on the contrary, to a restricted number either for purposes of preferential promotion or to help them cope with specific problems.

2. General Capital Access Measures Open to All SMB's

Generally, an organisation more or less linked with the Government grants credit facilities and, at the same time, necessary advice on their use.

In Norway, the Fund for Craft-Trades and Small Businesses, set up in 1914, had its field of activity extended in 1967. Today it assists in financing the investment projects of small firms by granting them guarantees and loans up to a maximum of Kr.500,000 in each case. In 1972 loans under this heading totalled about Kr.11 million. Since 1970 loans on concessionary terms have been available in Denmark to small and medium-sized firms. The amount involved under this heading is Kr.20 million a year.

Table 2

BELGIUM

SPECIAL AID TO SMALL AND MEDIUM-SIZED FIRMS UNDER
THE ACT OF 24TH MAY, 1959

(BFr. million)

	1970	1971	1972	1973	1974	1975
Total investment for which government assistance is given	5,238	5,742	8,165	12,927	10,089	10,425
of which total loans for which interest relief granted	2,080	2,049	3,232	6,028	4,587	4,057
Total assistance from loan insurance fund	895	1,340	2,022	2,763	1,876	2,414
Total administrative costs	185	190	344	776	553	504

In Belgium, under the Act of 24th May, 1959 on "The Enlargement of Facilities of Access to Industrial and Craft-Trade Credit",
the Ministère des Classes Moyennes (Ministry for the Middle Classes)
operates a loan insurance fund and grants interest relief. Table 30
summarises the Ministry's activities in this respect for 1970 to
1975.

In Finland, apart from the specific assistance to small and
medium-sized firms (defined as those with a turnover of under Mks.5
million) the Regional Development Fund grants loans and offers its
services (advice, information and technical assistance) which, though
available to all firms in general, are of special interest to the
smaller ones.

Under an Act passed in 1963, the government grants loan guarantees to small firms and Mks.2.5 million was earmarked in the 1974
budget for obligations that might arise under these guarantees.
Since the passing of the 1969 Act on interest relief for small-scale
industry, small firms outside the development areas qualify for an
80 per cent reduction during the first two years, and 40 per cent
during the next two, of the rate of interest on loans they have taken
out. This is conditional on the project having the effect of increasing production or workforce by at least 20 per cent. In 1974
new loans qualifying for this assistance can be granted up to a
total of Mks.25 million, the budgetary allocation for interest relief
in the 1974 budget being Mks.5.6 million.

Loans from the Regional Development Fund may be used for investments as well as for use as working capital. In principle, they cannot exceed 75 per cent of the total cost of the operation and are
granted for a maximum period of 20 years. In actual fact in 1973
they accounted for only 30 to 40 per cent of the financial resources
used and their average period was 9 years. The usual security is not
required for loans granted from this fund.

Sometimes a number of establishments share responsibility in this
field, each one specialising in a particular kind of credit facility.
Sweden and Canada are cases in point.

In Sweden, apart from the assistance provided through the
Business Development Associations, several institutions are involved
in giving guarantees, granting loans and buying equity, each one
specialising more particularly in one type of operation.

The Swedish business guarantee company (SVENSK FORETAGSGARANTI
AB), half of whose capital - which amounts to Kr.4.8 million - is
held by INVESTERINGBANK and SPARBANKERNAS BANK AB, had granted guarantees for a total of Kr.3,051,000 by the end of 1972.

The Industry credit company and the business credit company
(AB Industrikredit and AB Företagskredit) both grant long-term
loans - 10 or 20 years - using resources mainly raised from pension
funds or on the financial markets.

These two institutions, jointly operated by the government and the commercial banks, co-ordinate their activities. The former provides first-line credit (up to 60 per cent of the "coefficient of security") and the latter provides second-line credit (60 - 75 per cent of the coefficient). The loans granted by the business credit company sometimes carry higher rates of interest. About half the loans have been granted to firms with under 50 employees, who have received nearly one-quarter of the amounts allocated by these two financial organisations. The share of industrial firms in the total amount loaned is relatively lower than that of commercial or service firms. This trend is not peculiar to Sweden; it also occurs in other countries. In 1972 loans approved totalled Kr.790 million and money actually committed Kr.575 million. The figures for 1973 are Kr.816 million and Kr.831 million respectively. One-quarter of the amount loaned has gone to the mining, metal or civil engineering industries.

In 1973 an equity-purchasing company was set up - FORETAGSKAPITAL operated by the industry credit company. This institution is funded by both public and private money and has a capital of Kr.20 million. It uses the money mainly to purchase minority shareholdings but it is also empowered to give guarantees or grant loans.

In Canada, alongside the activities of the Industrial Development Bank, the Small Business Loans Act (SBLA) empowers the Government to guarantee loans up to a maximum of $50,000. This Act was brought into force in 1961 and has certainly facilitated the availability of credit to small businesses because since the inception of the act to the end of 1972, 27,207 loans amounting to over $259 million were made. Even so, the use made of this facility by small industrial firms seems to be diminishing as compared with businesses in the wholesale and retail trade and in the service sector during recent years. The share of manufacturing firms in the total of $11,190,000 in Small Business Loans granted in 1968 was 22 per cent, while their share in the $28,329,000 granted in 1972 was 12 per cent.

The Industrial Development Bank (I.D.B.),established by Act of Parliament in 1944, grants and also guarantees loans to small businesses. The bank operates in a decentralised manner and has an unusual policy with regard to interest rates. Through its five regional offices and 60 branches it has had contact with over 200,000 businesses since its existence. Since 1972 the bank has had an Advisory Services Department to promote good management practices in small businesses. In 1973, 117 seminars were presented to over 2,300 businessmen and 200 were planned for 1974. The mailing list has 10,000 names and addresses. Lower interest rates are applied to small loans and increasingly higher rates to larger loans where alternative sources of financing are more likely to be

available. From Table 3 it can be seen that the amounts loaned to
industrial firms have been falling steeply, in relative terms compared with loans made to businesses in the wholesale and retail trade
and in the tourist industry.

In Japan, there are Government-owned companies handling small
business financing operations: the People's Finance Corporation,
the Smaller Business Finance Corporation and the Shoko Chukin Bank.
The latter specialises more in granting loans to co-operative associations. Rates of interest vary between 9.4 and 9.9 per cent depending
on the period and purpose of the loan. Special loans at lower rates
are granted by all three institutions in special cases. During fiscal
1974, the ceiling for ordinary loans amounted to Yen 1,805,000 million, the total, including special loans, amounting to Yen 2,023,300
million.

There are also three companies, in Tokyo, Nagoya, and Osaka,
whose function is to acquire shares in small businesses. The
Government has holdings of 6.8, 13.9 and 6.2 per cent, respectively,
in these companies which take up shares in order to permit growth
and development in small businesses that would not otherwise be able
to obtain the necessary financial resources. The capital owned by
these companies on 1st April, 1973 was Yen 4,000, 2,800 and 4,200
million respectively. It is expected that the number of shareholdings
will reach 95 during the 1974 fiscal year.

3. Preferential Access to Capital

Apart from the general wish to help small businesses develop,
other considerations sometimes call for selective assistance or for
support which varies from case to case.

In Greece, government guarantees are higher for firms which export: for them the ceiling is Drs.8 million instead of the usual
Drs.6 million.

In Italy, location and turnover affect assistance granted in
the form of loan guarantees, loans at concessionary rates and participation. The main government agencies for this purpose are the
Cassa per il Mezzogiorno and the Istituto Centrale di Credito a
Medio Termine.

In Finland, in addition to its general functions (see above),
the Regional Development Fund is involved in the development of industrial estates, which are joint-stock companies owned by several
enterprises operating in the estate. In 1974, Mks.11 million was
earmarked for the loans to industrial estates. The Fund may also
acquire shares in a company temporarily whenever financing in this
form is regarded as important. There are three other specialised
credit institutions (the Finnish National Fund for Research and

TABLE 3

CANADA

TREND IN I.D.B. LOANS TO MANUFACTURING INDUSTRY, WHOLESALE AND RETAIL TRADE AND THE TOURIST INDUSTRY BETWEEN 1969 AND 1973

Type of Business	Fiscal year 1969		Fiscal year 1970		Fiscal year 1971		Fiscal year 1972		Fiscal year 1973	
	No.of loans	Amount (1)	No.of loans	Amount (1)	No.of loans	Amount (1)	No.of loans	Amount (1)	No.of loans	Amount (1)
TOTAL	2988	153440	3584	164628	4449	195980	5889	262310	7859	344798
Of Which:										
Manufacturing	798	52 011	737	50 954	991	55 625	1294	72 758	1495	79 671
Wholesale and retail trade	705	27 547	859	32 498	1081	37 109	1585	56 749	2149	76 986
Tourist industry	511	27 844	685	29 688	871	43 482	1209	59 340	1627	83 226

(1) $'000

Development, the Industrialization Fund, Ltd. and Sponsor, Ltd.) which have a certain importance in financing Finnish industries.

As an additional instrument in Finland one can also mention the financial support to firms in developing areas to compensate for the disadvantage consisting in the employment of untrained labour force. This support, which amounted to Mks.30 million in 1974, may be in the form of either an entirely repayable loan or of part-loan (at least two thirds of the total amount of the support) and part-grant not incurring repayment obligations.

In Germany, through the Reconstruction Fund which is currently being used to help national economic development, a number of measures have been taken in favour of small and medium-sized firms which, for various reasons, have claimed the attention of government. The fund grants loans on concessionary terms generally paid to financial institutions. These loans cover only part of costs, the remainder being borne by the firm concerned.

The Fund assists young businessmen in the distributive trades and in industry to invest, on the principle that the economy will thereby gain in vigour.

Table 4

GERMANY

PROGRAMME TO ASSIST THE ESTABLISHMENT OF BUSINESSES

1970 - 1975

Year	Number of loans	Average Amount per loan (DM '000)	Rate of Interest	Period
1970	1,605	27.0		(2)
1971	1,770	32.6		10
1972	2,383	29.2	6.5 % (1)	
1973	540	29.4		
1974	2,726	37.2		
1975	3,345	42.4		

1) 5.5 per cent for Eastern frontier areas.
2) 15 years for construction projects.

The small and medium-sized enterprises are, moreover, supported by the ERP Programme granting investments related to the location of the enterprises. This programme promotes enterprises which establish their plants in a new or reorganised district or which intend to relocate their plants to such districts. Moreover, the granting of investments for eliminating noise, bad smell and vibrations and, to a certain extent, the relocation of plants is promoted. In 1970 the

509 loans granted under this heading totalled DM.34.7 million. In 1971 the number of loans had gone up to 715 and the total amount involved to DM.59.2 million. In 1973, the number of loans dropped to 239 and the amount of credits to DM.15.2 million. In 1974, they strongly increased again to 832 and the total amount involved to DM.82.2 million. The corresponding figures for 1975 are 791 loans and DM.93.0 million.

In 1970, however, the Fund launched a more general operation and began to grant loans or guarantees to investment companies in order to encourage them to buy shares in small businesses. From a relatively modest beginning - only 11 participations in 1971 totalling DM.1.9 million - due to the reluctance of certain businessmen to accept outside help, this activity now seems to be gathering momentum, the figures for 1972 being 26 participations totalling DM.4.2 million, and for 1973 40 participations for a value of DM.10.3 million. In 1974 the participations increased to 61 and the credits to DM.15 million. For 1975, the corresponding figures are 45 and DM.13.4 million.

Regional considerations are also involved in the Fund's efforts to promote small businesses. Those prepared to set up, or invest in, the Eastern areas or other assisted areas qualify for loans. 2,439 loans were granted under this heading in 1970, the total amount involved being DM.254.6 million. The corresponding figures for 1971 are 2,437 and DM.244.9 million, and for 1972, 3,259 and DM.247 million. In 1973, a guarantee was given only for 363 loans totalling DM.26.9 million. In 1974, the number of recipients rose strongly, i.e. to 5,325, and the amount of loans to DM.387.7 million. The figures for 1975 cover 4,668 promoted enterprises and DM.340.5 million.

Assistance to small and medium-sized firms in the United Kingdom is available as a normal part of regional policy, but in addition there are special schemes which have been designed to improve the economic and social conditions of rural areas.

The Highlands and Islands Development Board makes grants and loans to any business which in the Board's opinion will contribute to the economic and social development of the area. Assistance can take the form of a grant or a loan and includes the power to provide assistance for buildings, plant equipment and working capital. The Board is also empowered to build factories for lease and has a programme of advanced factory building in hand. Since its inception in 1965 the Board has dealt with 2,300 approved projects creating nearly 8,000 new job opportunities at a total cost of £14.25 million.

The purpose of the Council for Small Industries in Rural Areas (COSIRA) set up in 1968 and the Small Industries Council for Rural Areas of Scotland (SICRAS) set up in 1969 was roughly the same. Apart from the provision of comprehensive advisory services to small firms, the Councils also administer credit services in the form of an industrial loan fund and a tourism loan fund. Firms eligible for these services are normally manufacturing and service industries situated in rural areas or country towns having a population of not more than 10,000 (15,000 in Scotland), and employing not more than 20 skilled persons. Agriculture, horticulture and retail trades are excluded at present. Loans under the industrial loan fund do not normally exceed 80 per cent of the cost of a project, with an overall limit of £20,000. The maximum amount any one borrower may be indebted to the Councils at any one time under the tourism loan fund is £25,000. Since 1968 £4,615,000(1) has been advanced from the Development Fund, administered by the Development Commission, to COSIRA and £372,500(1) to SICRAS for financing loan funds.

Unlike the situation elsewhere, industry's share in the loans made by these two organisations does not appear to be diminishing.

Table 5 shows the breakdown for industrial loans during recent years (in £).

Table 5

UNITED KINGDOM

COSIRA			
Year	Equipment	Building	Working Capital
1968/69	124,309	196,548	170,632
1969/70	48,550	239,822	181,240
1970/71	40,059	360,419	301,782
1971/72	83,327	706,357	330,743
1972/73	152,104	964,601	124,622
1973/74	154,262	1,177,088	294,454
1974/75	243,082	1,368,997	251,865

SICRAS	
Year	Total
1969/70	73,754
1970/71	106,099
1971/72	103,266
1972/73	81,761
1973/74	57,525
1974/75	146,606

1) These figures include amounts granted to the tourist industry.

Administrative costs for advisory and credit services put together are as in Table 6.

Table 6

UNITED KINGDOM

Year	COSIRA	SICRAS
1968/69	332,074	–
1969/70	490,962	123,772
1970/71	609,846	165,926
1971/72	739,916	208,585
1972/73	786,600	209,504
1973/74	887,600	229,116
1974/75	1,206,100	289,254

It is estimated that COSIRA has established contact with some
14,000 of the small firms within its sphere of activity.

A study made in 1971 showed that over 7 years, COSIRA and its
predecessors - the Rural Industry Bureau, Rural Industries Loan Fund
(R.I.L.F.) and the County Rural Industries Committees - assisted in
increasing employment in the countryside to the extent of some
27,000 jobs.

A survey carried out over the period April 1970 to March 1972
found that at a time when the total number of people employed in
Scotland fell by 4 per cent, the rural firms remained relatively
stable. Where SICRAS had been providing substantial assistance,
small firms showed a marked growth. The employment provided by 280
firms given concentrated assistance rose from 1,855 to 2,703, an increase of 45 per cent.

C. MARKETING

The marketing function is often not very highly developed in
small and medium-sized firms and the authorities have frequently had
to help in this area, particularly in relation to export markets.

As far as the home market is concerned, government action is
generally limited to advice or to giving small firms preferential
treatment in certain cases (cf. access to and participation in
government contracts).

The small size and limited resources of such firms often rule
out any possibility of setting up big sales networks abroad. They
naturally take advantage - and probably to a greater extent than
other firms - of government action abroad aimed at publicising national products and improving the arrangements made to market them.

One illustration is the Norwegian Export Development Fund which, since 1973, has taken over the activities in this field of the Fund for the Structural Adaptation of Industry. Grants are paid amounting to up to 50 per cent of the cost of marketing operations, which generally involve joint action by a number of firms. The Fund used Kr.9 million in 1974.

In Sweden, in addition to the activities of the Business Development Associations, mention should be made of the role of the Export Board. This was set up in 1972 in order to handle Sweden's commercial representation abroad. It also supports certain export operations. The Swedish Government spent Kr.8.2 million in 1973/74 and this figure is likely to go up to Kr.8.6 million in 1974/75. Alongside this general action, the country has also made specific efforts to promote exports of textiles and glass products, furniture, footwear and leather articles. Kr.9.1 million was spent for this purpose in 1973/74. The amount for 1974/75 is likely to be similar. It will be used for giving guarantees and grants and for paying international marketing consultants used by the recipient firms.

In Italy, in addition to granting loans at concessionary rates, the Istituto Centrale di Credito a Medio Termine has recently decided to provide insurance against the commercial and political risks attaching to short-term credit.

Japan, where a percentage of export turnover may be put to reserve, free of tax, and used to build up sales networks abroad(1), organises exhibitions to advertise and publicise the products of small and medium-sized firms.

D. ACCESS TO AND PARTICIPATION IN GOVERNMENT CONTRACTS

In view of the importance of government contracts in the national economy (in France they accounted for 7.4 per cent of the GNP in 1970), particularly in certain sectors such as defence, education and communications (when responsibility for the latter lies with the government), they can constitute a significant instrument of national industrial policy.

In competition with the bigger firms, small businesses could well find themselves excluded from this valuable market. Some

---

1) These percentages are as follows:

Commercial businesses:
- with a capital of up to yen 100 million: 1.7 per cent;
- with a capital of yen 100 to 1,000 million: 1.0 per cent.

Industrial firms:
- with a capital of up to yen 100 million: 2.3 per cent;
- with a capital of yen 100 to 1,000 million: 1.5 per cent.

In all, yen 5 million was spent under this heading in 1974.

countries, therefore, find ways of ensuring that individual small
firms, or all of them as a category, should have easier access to,
and participation in, government contracts when warranted by the
nature of the goods and services required and when the interests of
the nation so permit.

For the sector, new guidelines were adopted by the German
Federal Administration on 19th May 1976 for an appropriate participation of small and medium-sized enterprises from handicraft trade
and industry in the awarding of contracts under the regulations
governing the submission of tenders - excluding construction work.
The guidelines aim at distributing public orders on a broad scale
which are suited for small and medium-sized enterprises and at com-
pensating size-induced competitive disadvantages of small and medium-
sized enterprises in the awarding of contracts. According to these
guidelines, the authorities placing contracts are bound to invite
regularly also small and medium-sized enterprises to make a tender
in the case of restricted and unrestricted tender. Group bids are
to be admitted under the same conditions as individual bidders because thus the co-operation of small and medium-sized enterprises
can be promoted. Big orders are to be distributed in lots so that
the chances for a participation of small and medium-sized enterprises
are improved.

However, this illustration shows the limited extent to which
the government can help the small firm in this field. Public pro-
curement generally involves large-scale, standardised, and (in the
case of weapon system contracts), increasingly sophisticated production. From the technological viewpoint, small and medium-sized
firms are often not in the best position to meet such requirements.

Even so, under an Act passed in Japan in 1966 (Law Concerning
the Insuring of Small and Medium Entrepreneurs Receiving Orders
from Government and Other Public Agencies), the government endeavours
to increase the share of orders going to small firms as a result of
government contracts. Orders worth about yen 1,000,000 million out
of a total of yen 5,000,000 million have gone to such firms.

E. RELATIONSHIPS WITH BIGGER FIRMS

Small and medium-sized firms are often in contact with bigger
companies who sub-contract to them.

The National Sub-Contracting Centre set up in France in
October 1970 has framed a Charter which stresses the importance of
sub-contracting in a modern industrial economy. The specialisation
that sub-contracting promotes often results in a better distribution
of work.

Even so, between two partners of un[...]
ful is obviously likely to come off worse[...]
found it necessary to intervene in order[...]
of weakness in the situation of a small f[...]
company.

In France, the sub-contracting charte[...]
contractors certain considerations to bear[...]
lines that need to be followed if they are[...]
on a harmonious basis. In addition, specifi[...]
troduced in order to make sub-contracting mo[...]
on government contracts have been revised an[...]ractors.
A number of model contracts have been drawn [...]uring a proper
balance between the two sides.

The Japanese authorities have given special attention to sub-
contracting problems because of the very high number of small firms
involved.

Sub-Contracting Enterprise Promotion Associations — first
introduced in 1965 — now exist in 31 prefectures. These act as go-
betweens, issue information and give advice, e.g. by publishing
model contracts or order forms. In 1974 these Associations received
yen 100,000,000 from the government.

In addition, an act passed in 1956 established rules with regard to the relations between the two sides in order to bring to an
end certain practices including delayed settlement and insistence on
unduly high discounts. Checks are made to see that these rules are
observed. A designated subcontracting association, as provided by
the Sub-Contracting Small and Medium Enterprise Promotion Law, is
entitled to certain tax facilities and on 31st August 1974 three out
of the 36 approved assocations had taken advantage of them.

Finally, it may be added that, although running counter to the
rules of competition, concentration incentives, as we have seen,
may enable more competitive production units to be formed. They
also help to increase the bargaining power of the firms that join
together. Although generally this reinforcement of bargaining power
is not the primary objective in mind, it is nevertheless implicit
in the measures taken in this field in Germany, the United Kingdom
and elsewhere.

F. SIMPLIFYING REQUIREMENTS IMPOSED BY LEGISLATION AND REGULATIONS

Measures taken to simplify the formalities with which small
firms have to comply relate, among other things, to taxation, social
security contributions and various statistical information demanded
by the government.

special advantages are given to small and medium-
the assessment of taxable profits may be greatly simpli-
e them from having to keep over-complicated accounts.
of assessment on a presumptive basis exist in most countries
all firms.

In _Italy_, for example, one of the measures of tax reform provides that firms with an annual turnover of less than Lire 120 million may keep simplified accounts for purposes of direct taxation.
The amount of V.A.T. is determined on a fixed basis for firms with
a turnover of under L.21 million and on a simplified basis for those
whose turnover does not exceed L.80 million.

Small firms are also allowed to space out the payment of their
social security contributions. Apart from the simplification this
allows, the measure may also be designed to assist such firms from
the cash-flow viewpoint. In _France_, for example, employers normally
pay contributions every month but firms with under 10 employees pay
quarterly.

In the _United Kingdom_, the Bolton Committee recommended that the
government should reduce the burden on small firms of having to provide statistics and fill in various government questionnaires. It
also recommended that exemptions regarding the supply of certain information to the government (e.g. directors' fees) should be extended
to a larger number of firms. Action has now been taken on both
these recommendations to the extent that there is now a greater deal
of control on the amount of statistical information asked of small
firms and there has been an increase in the exemption threshold of
directors' fees etc. for which information needs to be supplied.

Chapter 8

THE FIRMS THEMSELVES

A. INTRODUCTION

Assistance to firms themselves supplements action taken with regard to the conditions in which they operate. There are quantitative and qualitative aspects. While increasing the size of the production unit may not be absolutely necessary for every small firm, it is nevertheless essential for many of them if they are to increase their ability to compete. Improvements in technology and management are often the key to survival. Even so, assistance designed specifically for small and medium-sized firms is exceptional and mainly relates to the qualitative aspect. In general, measures apply to all firms regardless of size.

B. IMPROVEMENT OF MANAGEMENT EFFICIENCY
AND MANUFACTURING PROCESSES

Alongside the assistance given to research in general, some countries have developed specific measures better suited to the requirements of small firms. They concern the improvement of management efficiency and manufacturing processes.

1. Management Efficiency

Measures taken under this heading include management training (discussed later in the report) and the use of consultants, the cost of which is fully or partly borne by the government. This form of assistance is generally much appreciated by businessmen: according to surveys made in Germany, for example, it is believed to make an important contribution to the technical and economic development of small and medium-sized firms.

In Canada, firms having fewer than 100 employees and no more than $5 million in sales are eligible for Counselling Assistance to Small Enterprises (C.A.S.E.) which started in 1972 in two provinces but is to be extended to the whole of Canada. The growth in the number of projects, which went up from 164 in 1972/73 to 243 in 1973/74, and in the number of counselling man-days (780 in 1972/73; 2,670 in 1973/74), indicate the popularity of the scheme.

The system in Germany is more graduated in its application, government assistance covering between 25 and 75 per cent of consultants' fees depending on the firm's turnover. Fees are set arbitrarily at DM.400 per day. Advice is generally given by the Economic Rationalisation Bureau (R.K.W.) which, in its turn, receives government assistance. The following table summarises the assistance given under this scheme between 1971 and 1975.

Table 7

GERMANY

PROMOTION OF BUSINESS CONSULTANCY

		1971	1972	1973	1974	1975
Federal government aid(1)	DM mil-	1.3	1.3	1.6	0.9	2.2
Länder aid	lion	1.3	1.3	1.6	0.9	2.2
Number of cases		1.326	1.308	1.427	1.452	1.415
Number of counselling man-days		6.953	6.736	7.737	7.893	13.564

1) Including money granted to the R.K.W.

In Sweden, in addition to the general R & D assistance programme, the Technical Development Office has spent Kr.7.7 million on its 1973/74 information and advisory programme. It is estimated that Kr.11.2 million will be needed for this programme in 1974/75.

Promoting the use of computers by small firms also helps to improve their management. In Germany, loans on concessionary terms are granted from the E.R.P. fund for the purchase of hard and software. In some exceptional cases help may also extend to the construction of buildings to house computer systems. The loan ceiling is DM.100,000 for one firm and DM.500,000 for shared use. The total appropriation under this heading has gone up by DM.5 million each year, having increased from DM.20 million in 1971 to DM.35 million in 1974. However, it fell again to DM.30 million and in 1976 to DM.24 million. The number of firms involved was 249 in 1970, 416 in 1971, 396 in 1972, 161 in 1973, 529 in 1974 and 638 in 1975, whilst loans totalled DM.15.6 million in 1970, DM.29.1 million in 1971, DM.3.7 million in 1972, DM.7.3 million in 1973, DM.21.9 million in 1974 and DM.24.7 million in 1975.

In Japan, subsidies are accorded to defray expenditure on facilities required for experimentation and study related to the adaptation of small and medium-sized businesses and carried out by local governments' experimental and research organisations. Half the cost is covered by the Government; in 1974 Yen 400 million was spent on 51 subjects of investigation.

2. Manufacturing Processes and Techniques

Here, government action is designed to provide the widest possible dissemination of information regarding available technologies and to assist firms in introducing new processes or manufacturing new products.

In Japan, groups of engineers and scholars are taken to see new technologies in action and the number of enterprises visited is estimated at 19,000 in 1974. In addition the government supports the cost of disseminating technological information on the widest possible basis through local organisations and spent Yen 23 million in 1974 for this purpose.

The Low Cost Automation Service introduced in the United Kingdom in 1968 reflected the view of the then Ministry of Technology that United Kingdom industry could benefit from much of the very simple technology available but not widely publicised. The cost of the service is £500,000/£600,000 spread over seven years. The service consists of advice, technical help, consultations, etc. in the field of simple mechanisation, automation and work study administered in 14 centres each one forming part of a polytechnic or university department. The service has continually changed its features since its introduction. These changes have not been orientated toward either a strengthening or a weakening of the scheme, but have been designed to enable the limited resources to be concentrated on those activities which were either most in demand by local industry, or were most efficiently provided by the centre concerned. It may be necessary to abandon the scheme in some areas since either demand has been insufficient or the centre has not been able to reflect the needs of local industry.

In Sweden, the Swedish National Development Co (SU), in addition to its general functions in the fields of environmental protection, medicine and public health, data processing and transport, assists small inventors and small firms to develop, produce and market new systems or processes. In addition, the Fund for the North of Sweden has been financing the Industrial Development Centre in that area since 1971 with an annual contribution of 12 million kroner. This centre contributes to improvements in production by analysing problems involved in the assessment of commercial and technical opportunities of new product ideas, technical testing and control, construction of product prototypes, etc.

In Norway, the activities of the National Technology Institute, set up in 1917, have been directed in recent years more especially, through its nine regional branches, towards helping small firms.

Its main tasks are to help in making new technologies known and in bringing them into use.

In <u>Canada</u>, the Technical Information Service (T.I.S.), established in 1946 by the National Research Council, has an important role.

Each year its field engineers visit some 12,000 firms and handle 18,000 enquiries for technical information. In addition, 3,000 enquiries are referred to the National Office for more in-depth work. The T.I.S. also has a mailing list of 4,000 firms that have shown an interest in receiving specific technical information on a continuing basis. Films, audio cassettes, and 80,000 technical briefs have been distributed in this manner. In 1975 T.I.S. introduced the Industrial Engineering Service (I.E.S.) to provide in-depth assistance in the solution of production problems. Last year, of the 868 firms receiving assistance from this service 508 were new clients. The percentage distribution of man-hours for manufacturing industry is as follows:

Metal fabricating	13.5
Miscellaneous	11.6
Food and beverages	11.1
Transportation equipment	10.7
Furniture and fixtures	10.5
Machinery	9.0
Electrical products	5.9
Wood, paper and allied	10.5
Chemical and allied	4.6
Printing, publishing and allied	3.3
Non-metal mineral products	3.3
Remainder	6.0
	100.0 %

In all, close to 100 professionals work for the T.I.S., about 20 of whom are involved with the Industrial Engineering Group, 20 per cent of whose time is spent providing a more general management counselling service. This aspect of T.I.S. work is to be integrated with C.A.S.E. at some time in the future.

Officials estimate that the ratio of identified accrued benefits to the cost of operating this service is 10 to 1.

In <u>Germany</u>, in addition to the efforts being made to disseminate more information, a specific attempt is being made to encourage R & D activities in small and medium-sized firms.

As part of their campaign to increase productivity, the German authorities endeavour to provide small firms with all the technical information they need through the agency of the German Economic Rationalisation Office (R.K.W.), the amounts spent for this purpose being DM.5.8 million in 1971, DM.5.4 million in 1972, DM.5.3 million in 1973, DM.5.6 million in 1974 and DM.5.9 million in 1975. To this figure should be added the amount spent by the Länder totalling about

DM.2 million each year. About DM.50,000 managerial executives are reached annually through this information service.

Since 1950, through the agency of the 80 co-operative industrial research associations the Federal Government has been prepared to make grants to small firms in order to encourage them to take the risks involved in R & D. These associations have over 8,000 small firms as member in 31 different industries. Over the last five years (1971-1975) 1,270 projects have been assisted involving an expenditure of DM.202 million. Over 50 per cent of the public money spent under this heading has gone to the following 4 sectors: steel and motor manufacture, metalworking, chemicals and refining, leather, textiles and clothing industry.

In 1974, DM.48 million were available for this type of assistance, which seems to be particularly well suited to small firms' requirements in this area.

C. CONCENTRATION, INTEGRATION, CO-OPERATION AND ASSOCIATION

Not many countries have designed systems specifically for small firms to encourage them to join together. They are covered by the general schemes of tax and financial incentives to concentration or co-operation.

However, in view of the special nature of small firms they perhaps have a greater need of information and advisory services enabling the owners to weigh up the advantages to be obtained and to overcome reluctance to associate themselves with others and thus reduce their personal influence.

At the international level, one may note the creation, in 1973, within the framework of the European Communities, of the Business Cooperation Center. This Center has a triple purpose: - provide enterprises with information on the economic, legal, tax and administrative aspects of cooperations and transnational integrations; - establish contacts between enterprises wishing to associate further; - indicate to the competent bodies of the Community the obstacles encountered in transnational association in the Community. The most active sectors have so far been: chemicals, metal products, mechanical engineering and food.

In some countries, however, assistance has been aimed in particular at small firms wishing to join together either as part of sectoral policy measures (the most frequent case) or through programmes confined solely to small and medium-sized firms.

In Sweden, for example, restructuring aids directed at the textile, clothing, glass, furniture and footwear industries have largely affected small firms which are particularly numerous in these industries. The hiring of consultants is an essential part of these programmes. Apart from grants for this purpose, loans and guarantees are also available.

In Germany, projects of small and medium-sized enterprises which may be indicative of further co-operation projects of other enterprises are promoted under the ERP Programme for apprenticeships and co-operation. In this way they retain their independence whilst improving their long-term competitive situation. Moreover, the funds are designed to create (additional) industrial apprenticeships in recognised trades. The main objective of these supporting measures is to increase lastingly the productivity of the industrial enterprises through rationalisation possibilities inherent in co-operation ventures. Apart from that, the aim is to combat unemployment of young people. The Reconstruction Fund (ERP) grants loans for this purpose. The relevant appropriations in its budget were DM.10 million in 1973, 1974 and 1976 (and DM.7 million in 1975). In 1974, two measures were promoted so far at a credit amount of DM.0.1 million.

In Japan, the government endeavours to promote pooling arrangements and co-operation between small industrial or commercial firms by both fiscal and financial measures.

Businessmen, for example, belonging to a trade association can take additional depreciation, over and above their ordinary depreciation, equal to half of the latter for all capital expenditure on machinery, plant and buildings whose purpose is to modernise their production structures. This additional depreciation facility for small firms extends over 5 years. It was introduced in 1969 by the Small and Medium Enterprise Modernisation Promotion Law. In fiscal 1973, 11 new modernisation projects were approved.

In order to mitigate the difficulties of small retailers and to enable them to meet competition from large stores by forming associations, the Small and Medium Retail Business Promotion Law allows them to make a deduction, for tax purposes, of 10 per cent of the cost of equipment intended for joint use. This arrangement was to apply for two years as from 1st April, 1973.

The formation of reserves intended to be put to joint use by recognised associations is also assisted in Japan by a special fiscal arrangement in their favour. Payments made to associations are deductible for tax purposes and the latter are allowed to deduct the amounts they transfer to the reserve fund. This double deduction possibility was introduced in 1966 for 8 years and extended for a further 2 years in 1974.

Alongside these fiscal measures the Small and Medium Business Promotion Corporation, set up in 1967, grants loans free of interest or at very low rates (0 per cent in the case of activities for the promotion of unification of small factories, 2.6 per cent in the case of structural strengthening activities in the textile industry, 2.7 per cent for grouping factories, etc.) in order to deal with problems due to regional overcrowding and for the unification and re-grouping of factories. Since 1974 the Corporation has been financing loans for the advance buying of land and for knowledge-intensive activities. During fiscal 1974, Yen 91,000 million were invested in this organisation, in particular by the Government, for these purposes.

Chapter 9

MANPOWER RESOURCES

A. INTRODUCTION

In many countries, efforts made in this area relate mainly to
management training. The employment of highly-skilled manpower is
not a specifically small-firm problem. Specialised manpower training policies designed specifically for small firms are rare. They
are usually introduced on a more general basis with all manpower resources in mind regardless of the firm involved. They make an important contribution to occupational mobility and have been described
in Part II of this study. In Japan, however, the difficulty experienced by small firms in recruiting good engineers has induced
the government to organise engineer training. Each prefecture and
each appointed town (Kyoto for 1973) organises courses for engineers
in co-operation with industry and the universities. In 1974 Yen 97
million was allocated for this purpose and it was expected that the
courses would be attended by 8,000 people.

B. MANAGEMENT TRAINING

The methods used are generally similar from country to country:
courses, books, seminars and the use of audio-visual facilities.
Training is often incorporated in the activities of organisations
providing information and advice. The National Technology Institute
in Norway, the Business Development Associations in Sweden and the
Industrial Development Bank in Canada all have programmes for training businessmen in dealing with management problems.
In addition, special management training measures have been
adopted in certain countries specifically for small and medium-sized
firms.
In Sweden, since 1st July, 1974, the responsibility for most of
the government training programme has rested with the National
Swedish Industrial Board.
In Germany, the Federal government spent DM.1 million in
1971, DM.1.1 million in 1972, DM.1.3 million in 1973,
DM.1.5 million in 1974 and 1.8 million in 1975 on the development

of training and further training as part of its campaign to improve productivity. These sums went to private or industrial associations and to the German Economic Rationalisation Board (R.K.W.). The Board organises per annum about 800 courses of several days each attended by a total of 30,000 managers.

In Canada the 1962 Business Management Training Program was dormant during the late 1960's but was reactivated in fiscal 1971-1972 with a budget of $260,000. With this sum, about 20,000 students have been able to follow courses (available in English and French) during the last few years. The Provinces of Ontario and Quebec are also active in the development of courses in these areas. The plan is that responsibility for this programme will be assumed by the proposed Federal Business Development Bank, the setting up of which has been postponed because of the dissolution of Parliament.

In Japan, two training systems exist alongside each other. Firstly, there are teams of management specialists available for small and medium-sized firms in each prefecture. During 1974, Yen 1,333 million were spent by the government on running this service and the number of courses offered has been estimated at 43,000. Secondly, there are management consultants with the regional commercial and industrial organisations who also help owners of small businesses. In fiscal 1972 Yen 11,223 million has been spent to this end, 3,511,588 items of guidance supplied, 1,551,368 visits organised and 1,960,000 consultations arranged with the organisations concerned.

In addition, during fiscal 1973, the People's Finance Corporation granted loans on concessionary terms(1) for the carrying-out of restructuring projects recommended by the consultants. Yen 1,200 million were loaned under this heading.

---

1) Rate of interest: 7 per cent
   Loan ceiling: Yen 2 million (Yen 500,000 for plant and machinery);
   Maturity: 2 years (sometimes 3).

Part IV

<u>ANNEXES</u>

TECHNICAL NOTES

The tables below regroup, on a country by country basis, the
main quantitative information transmitted by countries in reply to
questionnaires I and II. They cover consequently the information
examined in Parts I and II of the report as well as the data per-
taining to instruments concerning small and medium-sized enterprises
examined in Part III.

The exchange rates used to convert the sums into US dollars
correspond to the rates used by the Statistical Service of the
Organisation for the conversion of foreign trade statistics. In
those cases where given information covers several years, a simple
average of annual exchange rates has been used.

In all the tables the sign . indicates a decimal point.

GERMANY
FISCAL AND FINANCIAL ASSISTANCE

Figures in million DM
(in brackets the equivalent in $)

Instruments		Object, identification of measures	1971	1972	1973	1974	1975	1976
FISCAL	Accelerated depreciation	Increases mobility of means of production	285 (81.9)	285 (88.5)	285 (106.3)	285 (110.0)	285 (115.9)	285
FISCAL	Accelerated depreciation	Promote investments in disadvantaged areas	290 (83.3)	320 (99.4)	340 (126.9)	480 (185.3)	555 (225.6)	650 (253.2)
FISCAL	Accelerated depreciation	Encourage R & D activities	130 (37.4)	135 (41.9)	140 (52.2)	145 (56.0)	-	
FISCAL	Fiscal Aids	Encourage R & D activities (investment grants)	140 (40.2)	155 (48.1)	215 (80.2)	240 (92.7)	85 (34.6)	
FISCAL	Fiscal Aids	Promote investments in disadvantaged areas (investment grants)	486 (139.7)	665 (206.5)	664 (247.8)	800 (308.9)	579 (235.4)	
FISCAL	Fiscal Aids	Promote investments in disadvantaged areas	532 (152.9)	532 (165.2)	532 (198.5)	532 (205.4)	588 (229.0)	588 (229.1)
FINANCIAL	GRANTS	Promote primary innovation			38 (12.9)			
FINANCIAL	GRANTS	Develop civil aircraft	190 (54.6)	210 (65.2)	214.5 (80.0)	240 (92.7)	279 (113.4)	
FINANCIAL	GRANTS	Encourage R & D activities in data processing sector (2)		109 (34.9)		37 (14.3)	48 (19.5)	
FINANCIAL	GRANTS	Encourage R & D activities in data processing sector (3)		589 (188.2)		220 (84.9)	279 (113.4)	
FINANCIAL	GRANTS / EMPLOYMENT – S R	Income guarantees for employed persons (4)	941.6 (270.6)	904.4 (280.9)	584.6 (218.1)	1209.8 (467.1)		
FINANCIAL	EMPLOYMENT – M K	Encourage geographical and occupational mobility	901.1 (258.9)	814.2 (252.9)	729.6 (272.2)	756.5 (292.1)		
FINANCIAL	EMPLOYMENT – M W	Other incentives for the benefit of employed persons (5)	97.4 (28.0)	109.0 (33.9)	933.4 (348.3)	918.6 (354.7)		
FINANCIAL	EMPLOYMENT – E I	Productivity subsidy programme	1.3 (0.4)	1.3 (0.4)	1.6 (0.6)	0.9 (0.4)	2.2 (0.9)	
FINANCIAL	EMPLOYMENT – E F	Promotion of information schemes	5.8 (1.7)	5.4 (1.7)	5.3 (2.0)	5.6 (2.2)	5.9 (3.4)	
FINANCIAL	EMPLOYMENT	Promotion of training and further training	1 (0.3)	1.1 (0.3)	1.3 (0.5)	1.5 (0.6)	1.8 (0.7)	
FINANCIAL	EMPLOYMENT	Promotion of joint industrial research	41 (11.8)	35 (10.9)	41 (15.3)	40 (15.4)	45 (18.3)	48 (18.7)
FINANCIAL	EMPLOYMENT	Regional programme	175 (50.3)	180 (55.9)	205 (76.5)	217.5 (84.0)	230 (93.5)	343 (133.6)
FINANCIAL	LOANS – S	Programme to assist the setting up of business	85 (24.4)	97 (30.1)	125 (46.6)	138.5 (53.3)	158 (64.2)	225 (87.7)
FINANCIAL	LOANS – M E	Programme for housing estates	20 (5.7)	25 (7.8)	30 (11.2)	35 (13.5)	30 (12.2)	24 (9.3)
FINANCIAL	LOANS – E R	Co-operation programme (7)			10 (3.7)	10 (3.9)	7 (2.8)	10 (3.9)
FINANCIAL	LOANS – E P	Programme to encourage the introduction of electronic data processing	13 (3.7)	15 (4.7)	10 (3.7)	10 (3.9)	15 (4.1)	15 (5.8)
FINANCIAL	LOANS	Participation programme	14.6 (4.2)	-	14.6 (5.4)			
FINANCIAL	LOANS	Assistance to shipbuilding						
FINANCIAL	Guarantees	Promote investment in disadvantaged areas (6)	400 (114.9)	400 (124.2)	400 (149.2)	400 (154.4)	400 (162.6)	

1) Grants made by the authorities from tax receipts.
2) Market related technical development.
3) Industrial research, long-term industrial development work and new applications.
4) Short-time allowances and bad weather allowances in the building industry.
5) Almost exclusively directed towards the building industry.
6) Programme funds.
7) Programme created in 1973.

171

BELGIUM

INVESTMENTS CARRIED OUT UNDER THE ECONOMIC EXPANSION ACTS,
JOBS TO BE CREATED AS A RESULT OF THESE INVESTMENTS, AND COST TO THE STATE
1970 - 1975

	Year					
	1970	1971	1972	1973	1974	1975
Investment carried out: total (in billions of BF)	76.6	59.5	43.9	78.5	55.9	46.9
(in billions of $)	(1.5)	(1.2)	(1.0)	(2.0)	(1.4)	(1.3)
Jobs to be created: total (in thousands)	44.5	40.2	36.0	48.2	33.3	20.4
Investment carried out per job to be created (in thousands of BF)	1714	1480	1219	1627	1679	2299
(in thousands of $)	(34.2)	(30.4)	(27.7)	(41.8)	(43.1)	(65.8)
Cost to the State: total (in billions of BF)	8.5	4.9	4.1	8.1	5.6	3.6
(in millions of $)	(170.0)	(100.7)	(93.2)	(207.9)	(143.8)	(103.1)
Cost to the State as a % of investments carried out	11.1	8.2	9.3	10.3	10.0	7.7
Cost to the Sate per job to be created (in thousands of BF)	191.1	121.9	113.9	168.0	168.2	176.4
(in thousands of $)	(3.8)	(2.5)	(2.6)	(4.3)	(4.3)	(5.1)

BELGIUM

BREAKDOWN OF THE COST TO THE STATE BY INDUSTRIAL SECTOR

In millions of BF
(In brackets the equivalent in $)

Industrial Sector	Year					
	1970	1971	1972	1973	1974	1975
Mining and quarrying	17 (0.3)	6 (0.1)	48 (1.1)	71 (1.8)	15 (0.4)	5 (0.1)
Energy	5 (0.1)	9 (0.2)	13 (0.3)	-	11 (0.3)	78 (2.2)
Basic metal products	1 574 (31.5)	974 (20.0)	479 (10.9)	640 (16.4)	221 (5.7)	93 (2.7)
Fabricated metal products	1 993 (39.9)	754 (15.5)	1 736 (39.4)	2 130 (54.7)	889 (22.8)	618 (17.7)
Chemicals	3 531 (70.6)	1 756 (36.1)	506 (11.5)	1 799 (46.2)	1 990 (51.1)	1 287 (36.8)
Textiles and clothing	458 (9.2)	359 (7.4)	289 (6.6)	455 (11.7)	356 (9.1)	179 (5.1)
Food products	101 (2.0)	257 (5.3)	202 (4.6)	716 (18.4)	600 (15.4)	312 (9.9)
Wood products	100 (2.0)	76 (1.6)	119 (2.7)	320 (8.2)	287 (7.4)	108 (3.1)
Building materials	277 (5.5)	207 (4.3)	210 (4.8)	803 (20.6)	395 (10.1)	117 (3.3)
Other	409 (8.2)	480 (9.9)	535 (12.1)	1 164 (29.9)	856 (22.0)	848 (24.3)
Total	8 465 (169.3)	4 879 (100.2)	4 137 (93.9)	8 099 (207.8)	5 561 (142.8)	3 644 (104.3)

173

CANADA

FINANCIAL ASSISTANCE

Figures in million dollars C.
(In brackets the equivalent in US $)

Type of assistance	Object, Identification of the measures	1968-69	1969-70	1970-71	1971-72	1972-73	1973-74
GRANTS	Program for the Advancement of Industrial Technology (PAIT)				36.8[1] (36.4)	36.7[1] (37.0)	58.0[1] (58.0)
	Industrial Research and Development Incentives Act (IRDIA)				31.3[2] (31.0)	32.1[2] (32.4)	30.1[2] (30.1)
	Industrial Research Assistance Program (IRAP)		7.5[1] (7.4)	8.2[1] (8.0)	9.7[1] (9.6)	12.6[1] (12.7)	14.6[1] (14.6)
	Industrial Design Assistance Program (IDAP)				0.7[1] (0.7)	0.3[1] (0.3)	0.7[1] (0.7)
	Productivity Enhancement Program (PEP)				0.3[1] (0.3)	0.9[1] (0.9)	0.7[1] (0.7)
	Program for Export Market Development (PEMP)					2.1 (2.1)	1.9 (1.9)
	Canada Manpower Adjustment Program		←	1.0[5] (1.0)	→		
	Canada Manpower Training on the Job Program				50.5[1] (50.4)	60.6[1] (61.2)	
	Canada Manpower Training Program			289.6[3] (284.0)	328.4[3] (325.3)	343.5[3] (346.2)	
	Canada Manpower Mobility Program			7.3[3] (7.2)	8.9[3] (8.8)	11.6[3] (11.7)	
Loans	Industrial Development Bank (IDB)		153.4 (151.9)	164.6 (161.4)	196.0 (194.1)	262.3 (264.8)	344.8 (344.6)
	General Adjustment Assistance Program (GAAP)				19.9[4] (19.7)	15.7[4] (15.8)	10.8[4] (10.8)
Guarantee	Small Business Loans Act	11.2[6] (11.1)	16.3[6] (16.1)	13.8[6] (13.5)	22.3[6] (22.1)	28.3[6] (28.6)	
Financial assistance [7]	Defense Industry Program (DIP)				48.8[3] (48.3)	48.3[3] (48.8)	57.5[3] (57.5)

1) Funds committed.

2) Grants authorized.

3) Funds expended.

4) Total of loan guarantees.

5) From 1965, year of creation of the program, to 1972-73, total of the Federal Contribution to completed programs, although the accounts have not yet been closed. The Federal contribution to assessment agreements in progress is estimated at 0.6 million $ C.

6) Calendar year.

7) Assistance may be in the form of grants or loans. No breakdown into these two forms is available.

ASSISTANCE TO INDUSTRIAL ENTERPRISES

Figures in million F
(In brackets the equivalent in $)

Type of assistance		Object, identification of assistance	1972	1973	1974
Tax aid		Tax authorisation for regional development (1)	54.90(2) (10.7)	76.83(2) (18.3)	63.80(2) (12.2)
		For the restructuring of enterprises	29.34(2) (5.7)	17.49(2) (4.2)	15.07(2) (2.9)
		For the development in foreign countries	n.a. n.a.	n.a. n.a.	1.29(2) (0.2) 300.00(7) (57.5)
		Assistance for the development of overseas "departments"	17.83(2) (3.5)	40.03(2) (9.6)	75.09(2) (14.4)
Financial assistance	G	Regional development grants	274.86 (53.8)	422.72 (100.9)	391.96 (75.1)
	G	Grants for the location of tertiary activities	10.44 (2.0)	4.89 (1.1)	18.20 (3.5)
	G	Grants for the location of research activities	-	-	0.41 (0.1)
	G	Decentralisation premium	26.90 (5.3)	31.70 (7.6)	31.5 (6.0)
	G	Vocational retraining grants	n.a.	n.a.	n.a.
	G	The "centime" for the South West and the "Franc" for Britanny	15.70 (3.1)	8.36 (2.0)	8.10 (1.6)
	G	Assistance for the development of overseas "departments"	32.34(8) (6.3)	27.55(8) (6.6)	34.71(8) (6.7)
	P	ESDF - Loans to industrial enterprises	489.35 (95.8)	883.42 (210.9)	2 379.92 (456.3)
		of which: Mechanical engineering Plan	12.50 (2.4)	50.40 (12.0)	16.50 (3.2)
		Iron and Steel Plan	370.00 (72.4)	530.00 (126.5)	760.00 (145.7)
		"Calcul" Plan	70.00 (13.7)	70.00 (16.7)	70.00 (13.4)
		Decentralisation actions	28.80 (5.6)	18.00 (4.3)	4.00 (0.8)
		Equipment and conversion actions	8.05 (1.6)	215.02 (51.3)	77.42 (14.8)
		Restructuring of the automobile industry			1 450.00 (278.0)
		Restructuring of industrial enterprises			2.00 (0.4)
	G/AR	Industrial policy appropriations (6)	107.15(3) (21.0)	105.79(3) (25.3)	176.69(4) (33.9)
	G	The Research Fund	n.a.	n.a.	210.83(3) (40.4)
	AR	The predevelopment assistance	8.80(3) (1.7)	10.50(3) (2.5)	13.63(3) (2.6)
	G	The development assistance	196.7(3)(4) (38.5)	159.7(3)(4) (38.1)	243.2(3)(4) (46.6)
	G ME	Assistance for the reduction of industrial pollution A. The Research Fund	1.72 (0.3)	3.20 (0.8)	3.96 (0.8)
		B. The Action Fund	1.10 (0.2)	3.30 (0.8)	2.07 (0.4)
		C. Assistance for the payment of dues	4.51 (0.9)	0.60 (0.1)	0.71 (0.1)

.../

ASSISTANCE TO INDUSTRIAL ENTERPRISES

(continued)

Figures in million F
(In brackets the equivalent in $)

Type of assistance		Object, identification of assistance	1972	1973	1974
Financial	G	Assistance to shipbuilding	654.70 (128.1)	710.61 (169.6)	800.22 (159.4)
	AR	Assistance to the aeronautical industry:			
	"	A. Development of new aircrafts	922.45 (180.5)	1 495.70 (357.0)	868.79 (166.6)
	"	B. Marketing aid	47.00 (9.2)	47.00 (11.2)	47.00 (9.0)
	"	C. Prospecting aid	2.42 (0.5)	3.27 (0.8)	3.87 (0.7)
		Loans to SNIAS[a] and SNECMA[b]		715.00(5) (147.8)	
	P	Assistance to the agricultural and food industries: A. National Forest Fund	13.57 (2.7)	14.28 (3.4)	16.50 (3.2)
	G	B. Prophylactic measures	0.06 (0.001)	0.11 (0.003)	0.19 (0.04)
	G	C. Agriculture orientation grants	177.93 (34.8)	179.67 (42.9)	196.45 (37.7)
	ME	Assistance to the informatic and electronic industry:			
	"	A. Calcul Plan	261.00 (51.1)	220.00 (52.5)	413.00 (79.2)
	"	B. Component Plan and Professional civil Electronics Plan	15.00 (2.9)	86.50 (20.6)	29.00 (5.6)
	G	Assistance to the oil industry	241.64 (47.2)	216.75 (51.7)	n.a.
	G (9)	Assistance to the film industry	126.04 (24.7)	147.56 (35.2)	178.25 (34.2)
	G	Assistance for the purchase of printing equipment	8.65 (1.7)	10.01 (2.4)	6.44 (1.2)
		Assistance to the newsprint manufacturers	14.80 (2.9)	13.93 (3.3)	19.27 (3.7)
	P	Specialised institutions: - Crédit National	3.31 (0.6)	3.80 (0.9)	4.73 (0.9)
		- Caisse Centrale de Crédit Hôtelier Commercial et Industriel	1.10 (0.2)	1.85 (0.4)	2.07 (0.4)
		- Caisse Centrale de Crédit Coopératif	n.a.	n.a.	n.a.
	P	Regional Development Companies(10)		1.30 (0.3)	1.00 (0.2)

1) Excluding the temporary exemption from the professional tax (patente).

2) Cost for the State.

3) Programme authorisations.

4) Reimbursements - 1972: 6.06, 1973: 19.8, and 1974: 20.4.

5) Total of loans granted 31st December, 1974.

6) The lending conventions include either the stipulation of reimbursement modalities or a participation by the State in the results.

7) Tax reductions in the oil sector only resulting from authorisations granted before 1974.

8) Major and growing share of the total (1972: 61.5 % to 1974: 81.8 %) has been granted to assist in the investment necessary for the production and distribution of electricity.

9) With the exception of selective assistance: 1972: 6.34; 1973: 11.02; and 1974: 14.15 which takes the form of an advance on receipts, the reimbursements have evolved as follows: 1972: 2.10; 1973: 1.40 and 1974: 2.10.

10) Contributions to the financing at long-term investments (public funds excluded).

KEY: G = Grant.
      AR = Reimbursable advance.
      ME = Research contract.
      P = Loan.

(a) Société Nationale Industrielle et Aérospatiale.
(b) Société Nationale d'Etude et de Construction de Moteurs d'Aviation.

ITALY

FINANCIAL INSTRUMENTS

In billions of lira
(In brackets the equivalent in million $)

Instruments	Object, identification of measures	State allocation
Grants	Act No. 1115 of 5.11.68 - Income guarantees	20 (for 1974 and 1975) (30.8)
Loans at preferential rates	Act No. 1470 of 18.12.61 - Assistance for Structural adaptations of S.M.B.'s	113 (173.8)
	Act No. 1101 of 1.12.71 - Restructuring of Textiles industry (1)	210 (322.9)
	Act No. 184 of 22.3.71 - Restructuring of firms	40 (61.5)
Interest subsidies	Act No. 623 of 30.7.59 - Structural adaptation	1 181 (1 816.1)
Financial aid	Act No. 1089 of 25.10.68 - Applied research and industrial development	250 (384.4)

1) The benefit of this act was later extended to other branches of industry (Act 464 of 8.8.72).

UNITED KINGDOM

FINANCIAL ASSISTANCE

Figures in million £
(In brackets the equivalent in $)

Type of assistance	Object, identification of assistance	1967 1968	1968 1969	1969 1970	1970 1971	1971 1972	1972 1973	1973 1974	1974 1975
G R A N T S	Regional development grants (Part I of the industry act 1972)						8.1 (20.3)	107.3 (263.0)	212.8 (510.4)
	Regional Selective Assistance (Section I of the Industry Act)						1.6 (4.0)		5.5 (13.2)
	Wool Textile Scheme (Section 8 of the Industry Act 1972)								2.6 (6.2)
	Other Industry Schemes (Section 8 of the Industry Act 1972)								0.7 (1.7)
	Mineral exploration and investment grant act 1972						0.1 (0.3)		
	Industrial expansion act 1964 - International Computers Ltd.	←———	13.5 (37.0)		———→				
	Current expenses grant	←——				14.9 (39.0)	—→		—→
	Regional Employment Premium	34.0 (163.5)	120.0 (244.6)	108.0 (259.0)	108.0 (259.0)	108.0 (263.4)	100.0 (250.0)	106.0 (259.8)	154.0 (369.3)
	Employment transfer - Key worker - Nucleus Labour Force Schemes		0.6 (1.4)	0.7 (1.7)	0.9 (2.2)	1.6 (3.9)	4.4 (11.0)	4.6 (11.3)	4.4 (10.6)
	Industrial development act 1966	314.9 (1513.9)	479.9 (1150.8)	586.8 (1407.2)	586.7 (1407.0)	491.5 (1198.8)	336.3 (840.9)	230.7 (565.4)	118.9 (285.2)
	Low cost automation service	←——			0.5 (1.3)			—→	
	Small firms, information centre service							0.4 (1.0)	0.5 (1.2)
L O A N S	Regional selective assistance (Section 7 of the Industry Act)						←—— 35.3 (87.4) —→		35.9 (86.1)
	Section 8 of the Industry Act						←—— 1.0 (2.5) —→		4.2 (10.2)
	Industrial expansion act 1968 - Aluminium smelting	←——		63.0 (168.5)			—→		
	Industrial expansion act 1968 - Queen Elizabeth II liner	←——	24.0 (64.2)	—→					
	Council for small industries in rural areas		0.9 (2.2)	1.0 (2.4)	1.3 (3.1)	1.9 (4.6)	1.6 (4.0)	2.0 (4.9)	2.3 (5.5)
	Small industries council for rural areas of Scotland			0.1 (0.2)	0.2 (0.5)	0.1 (0.2)	0.1 (0.3)	0.1 (0.2)	0.2 (0.5)
SHARE HOLDING	Section 8 of the Industry Act						←—— 5.3 (13.1) —→		3.5 (8.4)
	Industrial expansion act 1968 - International Computers Ltd.	Government took 10% equity stake							
GUARANTEES	Regional selective assistance - Section 7 of the Industry act						←—— 9.0 (22.3) —→		8.0 (19.2)
INTEREST SUBSIDY	Regional selective assistance - Section 7 of the industry act						←—— 27.4 (67.8) —→		25.3 (60.7)
FINANCIAL AID	Regional selective assistance - Section 7 of the industry act(1)						←—— 71.10 (176.0) —→		
	Science and Technology act 1965 - International Computers Ltd.					←——	40.0(2) (98.5)	—→	
	Industrial expansion act 1968 - Concorde production	←——		100.0 (267.5)			—→		
	Highlands and Islands development Board			2.3 (5.5)	2.3 (5.5)	2.3 (5.6)	2.3 (5.8)	2.3 (5.6)	2.3 (5.5)

1) Assistance outside general framework and including shipbuilding industry.

2) Up to this amount available to ICL between 1972 and 1976.

All figures rounded to nearest £100,000.

SWEDEN

Figures in millions of Swedish Kr.
(In brackets the equivalent in $)

Instruments			Object, identification of measures	69/70	70/71	71/72	72/73	73/74	74/75
FISCAL			Special deduction for investments				400 (83.1)	500 (113.8)	n.a.
			Special deductions for R & D activities					160 (36.4)	n.a.
			Special tax on certain construction work (1)		- 4.5 -(0.9)				
FINANCIAL	GRANTS		Regional development	56 (10.8)	62 (12.0)	65 (12.7)	98 (20.4)	154 (35.1)	n.a.
			Assistance to transport			41 (8.0)	53.3 (11.1)	65.6 (14.9)	83.9 (18.8)
			Fund for Northern Sweden (Norrlandsfonden)	4.1 (0.8)	5.0 (1.0)	2.7 (0.5)	2.1 (0.4)	12.3 (2.8)	6.6 (1.5)
			Conversion aid - use of expert Consultants (2)				5.0(1.0) 1.9(0.4)	5.0(1.1) 5.7(1.3)	4.9(0.9) 2.6(0.6)
			Aid to firms in difficulty				0.3 (0.1)		
			Services to firms					2.5 (0.6)	4.8 (1.1)
			State programme of management assistance	3.3 (0.6)	4.3 (0.8)	6.2 (1.2)	6.5 (1.4)	6.6 (1.4)	6.3 (1.4)
	LOANS		Regional Development	197 (38.0)	317 (61.3)	268 (52.3)	276 (57.3)	570 (29.8)	n.a.
			Fund for Northern Sweden (Norrlandsfonden)	20.6 (4.0)	27.0 (5.2)	34.8 (6.8)	23.6 (4.9)	31.7 (7.2)	34.7 (7.8)
			Loans to crafts and S.M.B.'s	95 (18.3)	78 (15.1)	75 (14.6)	92 (19.1)	135 (30.7)	n.a.
			Loans of the Industrial Credit Company (AB Industrikredit)	290 (56.0)	512 (99.0)	599 (116.8)	574 (119.3)	830 (189.0)	806 (180.8)
			Investment Bank (Sveriges Investeringsbank AB) loans	552 (106.6)	567 (109.6)	706 (137.7)	1159 (240.8)	453 (103.1)	1158 (259.7)
	GUARANTEES		Facilitate structural improvements in certain sectors (2)				(8.3) 40 (2.7) 13	(6.8) 30 (5.2) 23	(6.7) 30 (3.1) 14
			Special guarantees for textile industry		7.5 (1.4)	15.0 (2.9)	22.5 (4.7)	22.5 (5.1)	22.5 (5.0)
			Loans guaranteed by the State	40 (7.7)	32 (6.2)	67 (13.1)	62 (12.9)	79 (18.0)	n.a.
			Temporary exemption from interest payment (2)				(0.1)0.3 (0.1)0.3	0.8 (0.2)	1.2 (0.3)
	FINANCIAL AIDS		Project participation on a conditional repayment basis by the Technical Development Board (STU)	89.5 (17.3)	117.8 (22.8)	123.0 (24.0)	141.7 (29.4)	181.2 (41.3)	205.0 (46.0)
			State Development Fund					30 (6.8)	30 (6.7)

1) This tax was also imposed in 1967-68 and at that time it brought in 5.5 million S.Kr. The minus sign (-) is used because the sum involved represents revenue for the State.

2) The first figure (upper line) is the amount allocated. The second figure (lower) is the amount actually disbursed or committed.

DIRECT AID TO MANUFACTURING INDUSTRY

In hundreds of million of yen
(In brackets the equivalent in million $

	Object, identification of measures	1974	1975
GRANTS	Promote R & D activities	42.4 (14.55)	45.0 (13.20)
	+ Support for studies and experiments	4.0 (1.37)	4.5 (1.32)
	+ Management counselling	13.3 (4.56)	16.8 (4.93)
	+ Management counselling for heads of small firms	112.2 (38.50)	168.9 (49.6)
	+ Counselling for the improvement of subcontracting	1.5 (0.51)	2.6 (0.76)
	+ Development of technical information	0.23 (0.08)	0.25 (0.07)
	+ Demonstration activities	0.97 (0.33)	1.07 (0.31)
LOANS	Japan Development Bank: (1) - Conversion of the manufacturing process in the caustic soda industries	406.0 (139.30)	390.0 (114.42)
	- Development of industrial technology	575.0 (197.29)	680.0 (199.49)
	+ People's Finance Corporation - Smaller Business Corporation - Shoko Chukin Bank	20 795.0 (7 134.89)	24 761.0 (7 264.26)
	+ Small and medium business promotion Corporation	910.0 (312.23)	1 152.1 (338.00)
	+ Management improvement for the SMB's by the People's Finance Corporation	1 200.0 (411.73)	2 400.0 (704.10)
GUARANTEE	Restructuring of the textile industry (guarantees accorded)	438.3 (150.39)	423.4 (124.21)
	+ SMB Guarantee Association (guarantees accorded)	23 782.0 (8 159.75)	35 077.0 (10 290.71)
EQUITY PARTICIPATION	+ SMB Investment Companies TOKYO (2)	40.0 (13.72)	44.8 (13.14)
	NAGOYA (2)	28.0 (9.61)	28.0 (8.21)
	OSAKA (2)	42.0 (14.41)	42.2 (12.38)
Other	+ State procurements contracts	1 005 000.0 (344 829.68)	2 062 000.0 (604.939.20)

+ Replies to the 2nd questionnaire - measures mainly or exclusively addressed to SMB's.
1) A part of its activity.
2) Their share capital.

FINLAND

FINANCIAL INSTRUMENTS

Figures in millions of FM
(In brackets the equivalent in $)

	Object, Identification of measures	1969	1970	1971	1972	1973	1974
GRANTS	Promote R & D activities	5.2[1] (1.2)	6[1] (1.4)	12.6[1] (3.0)	14.5[1] (3.5)	21.5[1] (5.6)	24.5[2] (6.5)
	Increase capital of public enterprises	107 (25.5)	75 (17.9)	180 (42.9)	125 (30.5)	91 (23.8)	
	Rural electrification						13 (3.4)
LOANS	+ Promote water pollution abatement investments						11[3] (2.9)
	Development area loans						150[2] (39.8)
	+ Regional development fund (loans to S.M.B.'s) ++						130[2] (34.5)
INTEREST SUBSIDIES	Act of 1968 – Interest subsidies on postal bank loans	20 (4.8)	20 (4.8)	20 (4.8)	20 (4.9)	20 (5.2)	20 (5.3)
	Act of 1969 – Regional development						29 (7.7)
	Act of 1969 – Assistance to S.M.B.'s						5.6[2] (1.5)
	Regional development fund (assistance to S.M.B.(s)						11[2] (2.9)
GUARANTEES	Act of 1963 – Assistance to S.M.B.'s						2.5[2] (0.7)

+ At commercial rates.   ++ At reduced rates

1) Value of contracts.
2) Amount budgeted.
3) First instalment of a total of 500 million FM (1972 prices) to be financed jointly by the State and the Postal Bank over the period 1974–1983. In 1974 the Postal Bank will make available loans for a total of 30 million FM.

AUSTRALIA

DIRECT AID TO MANUFACTURING INDUSTRY

In millions of $A
(In brackets the equivalent in $US)

Type of assistance	1972-73	1973-74	1974-1975	Difference 1974-75 1973-74
Assistance to shipbuilding	30.7 (37.5)	21.0 (29.7)	24.9 (35.8)	+ 3.9 (+ 6.1)
Programme for industrial R & D	14.1 (17.2)	15.3 (21.6)	15.4 (22.1)	+ 0.1 (+ 0.5)
Grants for farm tractors	2.8 (3.4)	3.7 (5.2)	4.0 (5.8)	+ 0.3 (+ 0.6)
Grants for refrigerated compressors	-	-	2.5 (3.6)	+ 2.5 (+ 3.6)
Grants for machine tools	0.7 (0.9)	1.0 (1.4)	1.5 (2.2)	+ 0.5 (+ 0.6)
Grants for books	3.0 (3.7)	3.4 (4.8)	5.0 (7.2)	+ 1.6 (+ 2.4)
Grants to promote exports and reduction of payroll taxes	58.3 (71.2)	68.1 (96.3)	87.5 (125.8)	+19.4 (+29.5)
Assistance to structural adaptation	-	0.1 (0.1)	10.0 (14.4)	+ 9.9 (+14.3)
Others	0.4 (0.5)	1.8 (0.7)	2.8 (1.6)	+ 1.0 (+ 0.9)
General Administration	0.4 (0.5)	1.8 (2.5)	2.8 (4.0)	+ 1.0 (+ 1.5)
Total	110.4 (134.8)	114.8 (162.3)	154.8 (222.5)	+39.7 (+60.2)

OECD SALES AGENTS
DÉPOSITAIRES DES PUBLICATIONS DE L'OCDE

OECD PUBLICATIONS, 2, rue André-Pascal, 75775 Paris Cedex 16 - No. 40.113 1978
PRINTED IN FRANCE